Quit Ye Like Men

QUIT YE LIKE MEN

by

JOHN W. PERRY

The Memoir Club

© John W. Perry 2008

First published in 2008 by
The Memoir Club
Arya House
Langley Park
Durham
DH7 9XE

British Library Cataloguing in
Publication Data.
A catalogue record for this book
is available from the
British Library

ISBN: 978-1-84104-193-3

Typeset by TW Typesetting, Plymouth, Devon
Printed by Cpod, Trowbridge, Wilts

Dedication

These musings are dedicated to the then Captain Superintendent of HMS Conway, *Captain E. Hewitt, RD, RNR, and Headmaster T.E.W. Brown, together with their staff, Executive, Scholastic and Pastoral:*

Brooke-Smith, Bayliss, Carter, Drake, Franklin, Hampson, Kingsford, Laurence, Moore, Murphy, Mylroi, Oliver, Owen, Preen, Sanderson, Skinner, Padre Turner and Vaughn,

together with their counterparts at HMS Worcester, *Warsash School of Navigation, and Pangbourne School.*

Contents

List of Illustrations   ix

Foreword   xi

Acknowledgements   xii

Preface   xiii

Proem: 'Quit Ye Like Men' July 1955   xv

Chapter 1 Overture   1

Chapter 2 School Ships   4

Chapter 3 School Ship HMS *Conway*   8

Chapter 4 First Term   13

Chapter 5 Third and Fifth Terms   27

Chapter 6 Sixth Term   35

Chapter 7 Outward Bound: Ullswater   43

Chapter 8 Indentures   47

Chapter 9 Transition   49

Chapter 10 The Indian Run: *Cannanore*   61

Chapter 11 The Far East Run: *Shillong*   88

Chapter 12 Mediterranean Cruising: *Iberia*   105

Chapter 13 The Australian Run: *Pinjarra* and *Strathaird*   138

Chapter 14 Mediterranean Cruising: *Arcadia*   160

List of Illustrations

Between pages 48 & 49

1. Summer Term 1955

2. HMS *Conway* – hard aground by Menai Bridge

3. Sad ending to a proud ship

4. Cadets, Summer term 1955

5. Cadet Holmes with ship's figurehead supine ashore

6. Re-masted ashore

7. Plas Newydd, with view of the Boathouse Tryst

8. 3rd XV rugby team

9. Sunday Divisions

10. The camp, post grounding of the ship

11. Upper Fifth Class, Spring Term 1955

12. Quarter Boys, Summer Term 1955

Between pages 80 & 81

13. Outward Bound – character building through adventure

14. King George V and Royal Albert Docks, London early 1950s

15. King George V and Royal Albert Docks early 2000s

16. s.s. *Cannanore*, deployed in the Indian trade-lane 1950s

17. Cadet Davie, starboard bridge wing

18. Cadets Perry, Davie and Paston, Colombo 1956

19. Andaman Islands, working timber

20. Wardroom of s.s. *Rajula* entertains officers of P & O, *Cannanore*

21. Christmas aboard *Shillong* at sea

22. s.s. *Shillong*, deployed in the Far East trade

23. Cricket in Penang

24. *Shillong* vs *Pinjarra* 1957

Between pages 112 & 113

25. s.s. *Iberia* cruising 1957

26. s.s. *Iberia* cruising 1957

27. Passenger Bridge Visit Day, s.s. *Iberia*

28. s.s. *Iberia* cruising 1957

29. 'Limousine' launch service for passengers

30. Invitation to cocktail party

31. Cadets' Cabin Steward 'Bif' Kemp

32. *Iberia* 1957, 1st Class Dining Room Gala Night

33. *Arcadia* 1958, 1st Class Dining Room Gala Night

34. *Arcadia* – back on the Australian service

35. Wardroom, s.s. *Arcadia*, cruising 1958

Between pages 144 & 145

36. s.s *Pinjarra*, deployed to the Australian trade 1957/58

37. s.s. *Strathaird*

38. Bombay circular

39. s.s. *Strathaird* 1958

40. s.s. *Strathaird* 1958

41. s.s. *Strathaird* 1958

42. Invitation to cocktail party

43. Skiffle group the 'Iberians'

Foreword

To many of us Old Salts, the 1950s and 60s were looked upon as the golden years of the British Merchant Navy. The UK fleet expanded rapidly following the destruction and the loss of so many fine ships and courageous seamen during the second world war.

During this expansion many excellent ships were built for all the major shipping companies that then existed and there were exciting careers and opportunities for the young men of the time in all aspects of shipping. One could sail into most ports of the world and find the majority of the ships therein proudly flying the Red Ensign.

My shipmate and lifelong friend John Perry has set out to record for posterity the life of an apprentice indentured to the P & O Steam Navigation Company, one of the great shipping companies of the time.

He has captured with great skill the atmosphere, the fun and the hard work we all experienced during pre-sea training and at sea, in our quest for success in the Board of Trade examinations that would enable us to become qualified professional navigators and seamen.

These were surely the happiest days of our lives!

Captain K.H. Davie

Acknowledgements

I am greatly indebted to all who have contributed to the contents of this book, in particular © English Heritage, NMR Aerofilms Collection for permission to use the photograph of the Royal Docks (AFL03/Aerofilms/A57), London City Airport for their photograph of the Royal Docks in airport mode, and Fotoflite of Ashford, Kent for photographs of *Cannanore*, *Iberia* and *Pinjarra*.

Additionally, to David Redman (Conway '53–'55) for his invaluable technical help in making other photographs reproduction friendly, and finally my wife, whose patient support has been constant.

Preface

In the 1950s, when Britain boasted one of the world's largest merchant fleets, shipping lines largely depended on pre-sea training colleges to provide a steady output of young men who sought to 'go down to the sea in ships', intent upon a sea-going career as navigating officers.

These Cadets, trained and disciplined in all matters nautical over a two or three year period ashore, sought thereafter to take Indentures with a Shipping Line of their choice, apprenticed thereto for a period of three years. This enabled adequate sea-time to be accumulated to enable them to sit the Board of Trade examination for Second Mate, a springboard to achieving officer rank and a hoped for eventual command.

The four most prestigious or well known colleges were HMS *Conway*, based in the grounds of the Marquis of Anglesey; HMS *Worcester*, moored off Gravesend on the Thames; Pangbourne College in Berkshire; and the School of Navigation, Warsash, near Southampton. The first two no longer exist, Pangbourne now only champions terrestrial academia, whilst Warsash (now Maritime Academy) uniquely continues to extol the virtues of its three year Cadet training courses, as part of Southampton Solent University. The demise, or re-focusing (albeit retaining strong Old Boy associations), of these centres of nautical excellence, together with the substantial loss of career opportunity for aspiring sea-goers, shadowed the steady decline of Britain's merchant fleet.

It was an extraordinarily vibrant period of our nautical history, now sadly disappeared, and *Quit Ye Like Men* seeks to bring a humorous and sometimes tongue in cheek portrayal of the period through the eyes and experiences of one such Cadet, graduate of HMS *Conway* and indentured to the P & O Steam Navigation Company, itself a once proud British institution but now only a shadow behind a brand of the American cruise ship company Carnival.

Factually, it traces two years at HMS *Conway*, the Naval disciplines, academia, the humour and frustrations, followed by a month of 'character building through adventure' at the Outward Bound Mountaineering School, Ullswater. Thereafter, a three-year span of apprenticeship with P & O, reflective of the style and substance of life for P & O Cadets serving in the so-called India run, the Australia run, the Far East run and, aspiration of all P & O Cadets, Mediterranean cruising. Nothing of that style or substance can be found today, and whilst one cannot challenge the professionalism that continues to exist, the fun has, most definitely, been driven out!

Proem

'Quit Ye Like Men'
July 1955

The elements were appropriately kind that day over North Wales in July 1955, and as the sun shone hotly upon the spacious grounds of the Marquis of Anglesey, so a cooling breeze blew in across the Menai Strait to bring some relief to the perspiringly uniformed Cadets of HMS *Conway*, wheeling sturdily in practised symmetry past the saluting dais. For some it was just the end of another term, but for that class of Summer 1955, it was their Passing Out Parade, and whatever the aspiration of each individual, the Class stood tall among the parade of five Divisions – Mizzen, Main, Forecastle, Hold and Foretop – that trod the hallowed grass of the *Conway/Worcester* rugby pitch, past the Captain Superintendent and Visiting Dignitary.

The bugle and drum band, inspired by hours of practice and illicit cigarettes behind the cricket pavilion, placed this time not a beat wrong, and not one Divisional Cadet Captain fluffed his 'eyes left' command at the saluting dais.

For one Cadet, this day held particular significance, and he marched proudly with his fellow Cadets. Privileged to be awarded the Queen's Gold Medal, he was to receive it from the hands of the Visiting Dignitary after Parade dispersal, no less a personage than Sir Donald Forsyth Anderson, Chairman of the Shipping Federation, but more importantly, Deputy Chairman of the Peninsular & Oriental Steam Navigation Company, into whose august indentures the Cadet had been invited to enter, a fairly unusual occurrence for a Nautical College so far flung from London. That the Dignitary was aware of the significance of this was without doubt.

Sir Donald, immaculate in his double-breasted grey suit and imposing in his distant looks and bushy eyebrows, accepted salute and offered his hand in congratulation to the tense Cadet before him, the latter painfully aware of the possibility that Sir Donald could yet see flaws that might, at the eleventh hour, question his Indenture to the P & O.

Sir Donald's words bore witness to his distant looks. 'Well done, well done, and what Company do you hope to join?'

CHAPTER 1

Overture

To those who aspired to become sea-going Navigating Officers in the 50s there were, as now, two alternatives, although the passage of time has seen each diminish as a career vehicle – entry as Midshipman to the Royal Navy via Dartmouth, or as Cadet or Apprentice to the Merchant Navy. The latter held a dual choice of means, either direct entry to a four year sea-going apprenticeship, or two (sometimes three depending on age) years at a pre-sea Nautical College, followed by a three year apprenticeship at sea with the shipping company of choice or dictate. It was a fact that of those that chose to go down to the sea in Merchant ships, a recognisable proportion were Dartmouth aspirants who had missed the Royal boat owing to age, background, or plain inability to pass the examinations (late developers), whilst others were uninspired by the thought of rust-streaked woodbine funnels or interminable association with the Merchant Navy's workhorses, that is to say cargo ships or tankers.

All was not necessarily lost, however, for the British Merchant Service in those days boasted an elite group of ocean-going passenger liner services, now sadly and almost totally depleted, with such famous names as Cunard White Star Line, the Peninsular and Oriental Steam Navigation Company, the Orient Line, the Royal Mail Line, Union Castle Line, Elder Dempster Lines, British India Line and others besides.

Of these, at least three imposed a tradition of discipline and uniform surpassed only by the Grey Funnel Line, as the Royal Navy was sometimes disparately referred to, with the obvious absence of weaponry, save perhaps the occasional animal 'humane killer', which scarcely rated in any arms race. Some of these further encouraged a percentage of their officers to seek Commission in the Royal Naval Reserve, and their vessels, where appropriately thus officered, to wear the coveted Blue Ensign, rather than the Red.

Of this group, one Company seemed to stand out from the rest, to be mixed-metaphorically described by one author as the 'Coldstream

1

Guards of the Merchant Service', its officers by popular myth entitled by some Royal device to wear a sword. Its white-hulled liners, whilst having no presence on the coveted North Atlantic trade-route, plied the exotic routes to Egypt, India and Ceylon, Malaya, Singapore, Hong Kong and Japan – or more westerly to Australia and New Zealand. They cruised the Mediterranean during the summer season, and the Line was very much a part of all that was seen to be the best of British Establishment.

It was, of course, the Peninsular & Oriental Steam Navigation Company or more usually referred to as P & O, originators of the class ticketing system 'Port Outward, Starboard Home', holding therefore pride of authorship in the word 'POSH' that has long been part of our language. So distinctly different was the company from other merchantmen that it stood apart in some solitary splendour, to the extent that it fuelled the myth in those halcyon days that Britain aspired to three Navies – the Royal Navy, the P & O and the Merchant Navy. The veracity of that tricorn state of affairs was in no doubt to those that officered the P & O ships, whilst to those that did not, the myth of the famous sword remained a constant enigma only heightened by the frustration of not really knowing!

Entry to Deck Officer service with the P & O in the 50s was almost exclusively via an Apprentice Indenture, Cadet Officers being required to prove successful completion of pre-sea training at a recognised Naval College, and more unusually, pass standards imposed during a month at the Outward Bound Trust Mountaineering School in the Lake District. Naval academia, discipline, and character breeding through adventure: a formidable trio of initial demands. 'QUIS NOS SEPERABIT' as the Company motto so succinctly questioned, the answer being almost rhetorical. Maintenance of quality would perpetuate the Line!

London based then, the P & O in the 50s boasted a passenger fleet of twelve vessels, carrying such famous names as *Stratheden*, *Strathmore*, *Strathnaver* and *Strathaird*, *Himalaya*, *Carthage*, *Canton*, *Corfu* and *Chusan*, *Iberia* and *Arcadia*, not to forget the *Empire Fowey* whose passengers comprised HM Forces, for she was a Trooper. Captured from the Germans during World War II as the then *Potsdam*, she in some small part perhaps recompensed for the sinking, during that self-same monumental naval carnage, of the *Strathallan*, newest of the

'Strath' class of passenger tonnage, sunk in December 1942 by enemy action.

From the more down to earth side of the fleet listing, those vessels devoted to the carriage of cargo and sometimes twelve passengers were vessels equally well recognised in those far off days, evocative in their names too of the trade-lanes that the P & O served – *Ballarat*, *Bendigo*, *Perim*, *Patonga* and *Pinjarra* for the Australasian route, *Shillong*, *Soudan*, *Surat*, *Singapore*, *Sunda* and *Somali* for the Far East, and *Cannanore*, *Coromandel*, *Socotra*, *Karmala*, *Kyber*, *Devana* and *Dongola* for India. Wild in the pack came the *Aden*, for she was, then, the only P & O vessel that did not carry Indian crew. Rated by popular vote as the punishment ship of the fleet, she was temporary berth for those Officers that had transgressed, to give them time to reflect on the errors of their ways and the depths of the 'pool' from which the so-called 'white crew' had been drawn!

All have now gone, victims of age (the *Shillong* died in relative youth in the Red Sea, her life fore-shortened by collision and sinking) and the *esprit de corps* that was so much a part of the P & O has disappeared, destroyed by the demands of a far more modern world, with its bottom-line pressures and changes in trade patterns. That the demands of excellence of those days are carried forward to modern shipping is without doubt – but what a lot of fun has gone away in the transition, as yet another era passes into history.

To go back to the beginning, however, those who aspired to join that Company of Empire had invariably to attend a pre-sea Training College, and those available then in the 50s have similarly faded into the sunset of more modern days. In a phrase, they have gone! Not victims of age, but of supply and demand. Gone! Late developing Dartmouth aspirants have nowhere, or almost nowhere, to go! QUIS NOS SEPERABIT? Bottom line economics shall so do! A shift of gear from sea to air travel brought about by the age of cheap passenger flights, and the never ending demand to run faster toward the ending.

CHAPTER 2

School Ships

CHOICE OF SHIPPING LINE was one that was not to enter the thoughts of many until well into their pre-sea training, but where to send young offspring to best advantage was, in the 50s, a fairly wide spectrum to be examined by parents. Merchant Navy Training Ships were then the spawning grounds for the Merchant Service, and were largely dependent for sponsorship upon those shipping companies that would in turn draw upon their graduate products to officer their ships. That they have now largely disappeared is yet another function of the end of an era and a way of life distantly heralded in those heady 50s, but unseen and unanticipated as the severe decline in the British Merchant fleet over the few decades to come thereafter.

There were four of top particular note, HMS *Conway* in the Menai Strait, HMS *Worcester* in the Thames, the Southampton School of Navigation in Warsash, close to Southampton, and Pangbourne in Berkshire. It was mainly from these that the 'sea-pups' of the 50s sought appointments as Cadets, Midshipmen or just plain Apprentices to the plethora of alternative shipowners, one day hopeful to become Master, and almost all would enjoy a life and experience no longer available on such a wide stage.

Choice there was, however, and Training Ship vied with Training Ship in much the same way as Public Schools (in whose listings they were included), to keep the pipe-line full and the fees rolling in. Brochures were glossy and full of promise. Rugby was extolled as character breeding and the pulling of boats together with sailing opportunities lauded as something not to be missed. 'Set in the splendid grounds of the Marquis of Anglesey' (Conway) vied with 'in the busy reaches of the Thames' (Worcester), and 'the sailing waters of the Solent' (Warsash) – Pangbourne continued to extol uniformed academia! Academic facilities were largely over-sold, benefits of naval discipline loudly promoted and photographs of smartly uniformed Cadets liberally scattered, to play upon the emotions of would-be

Cadet and fond parents alike. In comparison to today's sparse shelf it was a hypermarket of choice, and doubtless equally confusing in its plenteousness. Two years or three years of pre-sea training were also options, parental choice no doubt coupled to financial constraints (circa £80 per term was no small bread in those days, not forgetting uniforms and so forth) or desire to shuffle young loin-sprung to career earlier at fourteen years, or the less tender age of fifteen. To some the choice was pre-ordained by virtue of father's 'old boy' association to a particular college, and others by geography – 'why send the boy to Anglesey when we live in Portsmouth?' or 'to Pangbourne when we live in Liverpool?'

Current academic achievement was also impactive upon choice, and whilst 'Dartmouth failed' could probably contend with most Merchant Training Ship entrance examinations, school advice that Dartmouth should not even be attempted probably gave rise to more careful review of minimum examination percentages required elsewhere!

Thus, all over Britain, parents agonised with choice. In Sussex, one such family constrained only by the desire to do what was best for the boy and the County, and aware of advice from the local Grammar School that Dartmouth was not most easily attainable under current circumstances, decided that a Merchant Navy career was practically more available than a Royal, and grouped around various received brochures to choose. On balance, it was concluded that their boy would probably be enthralled by the prospect of rubbing shoulders with the Marquis of Anglesey, in whose spacious grounds resided the School Ship HMS *Conway*, and rugby, cricket, athletics, mountaineering, scouting and sailing were prospectus available. The Ship's motto, 'QUIT YE LIKE MEN' was adequately stirring, and no doubt distance would make the heart grow fonder! The amalgam of all these and other considerations indicated that HMS *Conway* was the way forward, and all that remained was to satisfy the College that the mental and physical capacity of the would-be entrant was adequate, and the Elders of Eastbourne that a substantial grant towards fees would be overall beneficial to the town. Elsewhere, others also chose *Conway*, whilst *Worcester*, Pangbourne and Warsash similarly won new intakes, and the game moved forward.

Uniform

The acquisition of school uniform is to this day a social facet of British life viewed with some puzzlement by more Continental Europeans. That it very shortly becomes the most scruffy clothing that a young person will ever wear becomes irrelevant in its uniformity, as it vaguely espouses the theory that an overall homogeneous school appearance will detract from individual privilege. For the uninitiated, such uniform acquisition for boarding school is usually frustrating, often exasperating and inevitably expensive in its sheer range of initial purchase. The 'kitting out' of intended boarders of a Naval College was all of those in the 50s, with the added worry that scruffiness was unacceptable and expensively corrected. An additional factor of some note was that naval tailors were rarely available within striking distance of the majority of those that sought their wares. Each Naval College had its 'recommended' tailor, and it was towards these individual establishments that anxious parents were directed, with lengthy lists of 'required' and 'optional' items. These were often necessarily purchased 'sight unseen', and supplied against sets of measurements put together by parents in doubtful partnership with sketched and written instructions.

So was it with HMS *Conway*, although *Conway*'s choice of naval tailors left southern (no doubt other) parents gasping in disbelief on reading that their offspring were to be uniformed by no less than the 'Liverpool Sailors Home', evocative of some tremble-fingered, bleary eyed beached tars sitting cross-legged in some Merseyside workhouse, as they plied their trade. A far fling from the more comfortable image of Gieves, S.W. Silver and Edgington, and Miller, Rayner & Haysom of London, more kindly recommended by HMS *Worcester*, Pangbourne or Warsash to their new intakes. Recognise, too, the doubt as to quality of tailors north of Watford, who surely could not be 'bespoke'!

Notwithstanding, and against all apparent odds, the 'Liverpool Sailors Home' did manage to creditably attire their young customers in their new guise as Officer Cadets, and sensibly recognised that physical growth would have to be accommodated over the coming months. That at least, and possibly euphemistically, was explanation for the final accolade of the tailor that 'it fits where it touches!'

Received via the postal service came the Naval cap with its gleaming gold braid badge of Her Majesty intricately woven, the double breasted uniform with gold coloured buttons and white woven Cadet insignia round the buttonhole of the jacket. Shorts, ties, rugby boots, sports shirts, blue battledress, oilskins, sea-boots, and all the paraphernalia necessary to identify with the exciting new life and to propel, in image at least, into the career that lay so invitingly ahead.

For all that, it would be an uncomfortably self-conscious group that was to assemble on First Term joining day, each looking, at the tender age of fifteen or sixteen years, vaguely ridiculous. To all intents and purposes, they were all attending a fancy-dress gathering, only to find that all had chosen to appear as Naval Cadets to the best of individual abilities, helped thereto by benefit of advice from fond, enthusiastic, unaware parents. It would be a beginning.

Anticipation

In far flung parts, forty some families agonised over forty some Cadets and their first departure from family hearth to their first term at HMS *Conway* – cabin trunk contents were yet again checked, tickets scrutinised, last advice given, uniforms twitched yet again into place, and last parental proud looks bestowed upon offspring about to bring to fruition all those months of speculating and planning: brothers and fathers envious, mothers and sisters tearful, and overall an immense sense of departure. In their turn, forty some Cadets preened their last mirror image prior to bus or train, ship or plane, and unanimously came to the single conclusion that a dash was most definitely cut. Each was to move toward nodule Anglesey slightly contemptuous of his fellow, civilian clad, traveller, and immensely conscious of his Naval uniform – equally, immensely unconscious of his immaturity, so obvious to fellow travellers! Sadly, and in common with all first term boarders, be they Naval or otherwise, each was blissfully unaware of his lowliness in the scheme of things to come, and each moved thuswise toward sharp disillusionment and swift reappraisal (slow in some!) of pre-conceived concepts.

CHAPTER 3

School Ship HMS *Conway*

HMS *NILE*, ONCE PROUD FLAGSHIP of Vice-Admiral Sir Alexander Milne KCB, RN, commanding the North American Squadron in 1862, became HMS *Conway*, and in the early fifties was moored off the grounds of the Marquis of Anglesey in the Menai Strait. In 1952, whilst en route for dry docking in Liverpool, she broke free from her tugs and took ground hard by the Menai Bridge, thrust there by the treacherous waters of the Swillies, that tidal maelstrom much respected by mariners. Unable to be pulled free she broke her back and after a thoroughly undignified paralysis was eventually destroyed by fire, having been picked clean by water and souvenir hunters. Her passing was no doubt seen as a sad loss by all those that had previously trained in her, but in reality was a blessing in disguise for those that were later to join the ship, reconstituted and encamped ashore in the grounds of the Marquis of Anglesey. Standards of academic achievement were to rise appreciably, and previous levels of bullying found on board were to drop to acceptable schoolboy proportions, in a shore environment. Those that served aboard may be forgiven for remembering otherwise, but so it was.

Now a 'stone frigate', the ship's motto 'Quit ye like men, be strong' and the sense of independence inspired by that demand was heightened by the Menai Strait that split the Isle of Anglesey from the north-west shoulder of North Wales. The tides ran strongly and oft-times dangerously through the Strait, and served as silent deterrent to those Cadets, unaffected by the legendary bromide, who listened to the Siren calls of Gweneth and Blodwin from Port Dinorwic, and thought to take a dinghy across to the boat-house so temptingly close across the water. It is said that a lusty few overcame that particular set-back to enjoy the favours of the southern bank, but reportedly the end, so called, only briefly compensated for the means!

Not all had changed, however, for it was essentially the second year Cadets who had lived aboard the old wooden-walls, the more junior being accommodated within part of the stately home of the

Marquis of Anglesey, a grey-stone ivy-clad building of imposing proportion, whose lawns rolled graciously down to the waters of the Strait. Here too resided the Captain Superintendent, renowned for possession of a powerful tripod-mounted brass telescope that afforded excellent search facility for Cadets smoking during boat activities, or indeed the occasional Gweneth devotee! The Headmaster and some four Executive Officers were also quartered therein, albeit in less imposing quarters.

The Marquis himself was seldom seen, and whilst it was strongly rumoured among excitable Cadets that he was mad, his choice of Marchioness would argue strongly for his sanity, for she was, by general agreement, beautiful.

Some few hundred yards to the north-east of the Marquis' home (irreverently referred to as the 'House Block'), and joined to it by a steeply winding, macadam roadway of indeterminate maintenance lay the 'Kelvin' or 'School Block', a battlemented and imposing building (once the stables of the estate) into which the academic life of *Conway* had been settled after the loss of the ship. Entered through an archway surmounted by an ivy-cloaked clock face, the courtyard inside contained 'temporary' hutment classrooms, which rubbed shoulders with the science labs and gymnasium.

On Sundays, the earthy direction of the Chief Petty Officer PTI would give way to the more pastoral admonishment of the Ship's Chaplain, one time marathon runner, as the gymnasium transformed into a surrogate church. Ghosts of horses past would stir uneasily to the resounding ring of the post-service rendition of the 'Conway Song', a rousing number that fell somewhere between the 'Marseillaise' and the 'Halls of Montezuma', sung as lustily by rote as the Lord's Prayer was mumbled.

Here too resided the 'Dartmouth' classroom, seat of instruction for those that still aspired, despite all indications, to seek entry to the Royal Naval College Dartmouth. Also, and more mundanely, were the showers and toilets that serviced the needs of not only classroom inhabitants, but also the residents of the 'Camp', newly erected to accommodate those Cadets displaced by the loss of the ship.

The 'Camp', a precise and geometrically established pattern of battle-grey hutments that now comprised accommodation for second year Cadets, was umbilically connected to the School Block by another macadam road that led therefrom to the north, and split the main rugby/cricket pitch to the west, from, at that time, fallow agricultural ground to the east. It was a triumph of planning, or perhaps a dictate of discipline, that the washrooms and showers for the Camp were so disposed in the School Block, requiring only a few hundred yards sprint each morning at reveille! 'Quit ye like men, be strong!'

Notwithstanding its ablutionary shortcomings, however, the Camp held pride of position to those arriving at Plas Newydd, for it lay tucked around, and hard to, the main road entrance to the estate, protected only from immediate view by the similarly grey painted cabins of the Ship's Chaplain and Chief Officer. The former, grim controller of Cadets' pocket money and patient advocate of God, the latter authoritatively but with equal patience, determined to turn his young charges into future officers.

Here, too, within the confines of the Camp, were quartered several Divisional Officers and members of the scholastic staff. Whilst the reason for their stabilising presence there was obvious, the positioning of their accommodation was perhaps unfortunate, as the occasional late night return from the Mermaid Inn at Foel, some 4½ miles from Plas Newydd, required them to restrain their own oft-times merry mood. In this they were at times delinquent and, as a matter of fact, more respected in consequence! The occasional instability of him who taught physics gave a new meaning and direction to the findings of Archimedes that he taught, whilst the dust of history was vacuumed away in knowledge that its champion in class was really a very modern person!

For all this, the focal point for both those that were resident and those that came to visit was the so-called quarterdeck of the ship, reconstituted ashore, just a few short yards from the main gateway. The imposing figurehead of the stricken ship was here re-masted, gazing sightlessly towards its ship's Menai grave, whilst the Cadet Captain of the Watch would stand importantly in front of his lobby and mark the hours. Behind him lay the office of the Captain Superintendent, four-ring Captain Royal Naval Reserve, known sometimes to wear carpet slippers behind his desk but otherwise imposing in his uniformed brusque authority and overall control of his sea-pups' destiny.

Last, but by no means least, there was the Dock, and this, as its name might suggest, was the point of entry to all things really water nautical to the Cadets of *Conway*. Situated to the right of the Marquis' residence as one viewed the Strait, it was approached by yet another winding narrow road that swooped down to the water's edge through sprawling banks of rhododendron bushes, to eventually arrive (in those days carrying groups of perspiring Cadets who had travelled thereto at the double and not unusually clad in cumbersome oilskins and sea-boots) to the Boatswain's store and sail locker.

From that rutted underfoot position would stretch the dockside for some 100 feet, curving right to the sea-wall and slipway, whilst to the immediate left, magnificent in its uselessness and tidal dependence, lay the so-called swimming pool, figment of some past misplaced imagination and no small cost. On the Dock reigned the Boatswain, a fiery Welshman, and here was the smell of hemp, paint and caulking, the very stuff of seamanship: knots, splices, blocks, whipping, sails and oars, and the ever pervading scent of the Menai Strait, a nostrum of kelp and decay, in nautical counterpoint to the truly pastoral scenery that was North Wales, spread in glorious section across the water of the Strait.

From and to here sailed and arrived the *Conway* fleet, gigs, cutters, Nos. 1 and 2 power boats, the Pinnace (late of the German raider *Potsdam*) and with luck and fair wind, the sailing craft. Here too drifted the smokers, to huddle around the dock-end toilets for the illegal drag (or 'spit' so-called). From this point of sometimes Sunday departure selected Cadets boarded craft that carried them, often damply, to church service at Llanedwen Parish Church, otherwise bereft of congregation, to worship. From the slipway, a starboard turn led past the sea-wall into the Strait, and a diesel-fumed lolloping, rolling run to the tiny rough stone seaweed-covered jetty opposite Port Dinorwic, and a short laughing march to the church.

To this then self-sufficiency in their seclusion, aspired some forty young men (or boys) in 1953, from places as diverse as Montrose, Scotland; Eastbourne, Sussex; Bangor, Wales; Melbourne, Australia; Dublin, Eire; Canada; Pakistan; and South Africa, not to mention Liverpool. What had drawn them all toward this outpost of North Wales in particular never really came into question, even in later years, although what drew them to a sea-going training never ceased to be cause for debate and reappraisal. Some no doubt had an unquestioned desire to go to sea, some came from broken homes, and some had family precedent. There were a perceptible few whose parents had no intention that Jack should become tar, but rather disciplined prior to a business career. As in all things, there were a few who should never really have considered it!

The class of Autumn 1953 were to come together, some to succeed, some to fail, some to demonstrate skills at rugby, sailing, athletics or whatever. All came to experience a two-year Naval training, a pre-sea course that would become history in their time, for *Conway*, like *Worcester* and many of the shipping lines that these Colleges serviced, was to fade quietly into the sunset of the 60s and 70s as Britain struggled to find her new identity in the 80s and far beyond.

Most would proceed to sea as Cadets, Apprentices or Midshipmen and most would go on to qualify as Master Mariner, and to command ships. Many would leave the sea before attaining the command that had first inspired. Most were to experience a life-style at sea that would largely disappear by the 80s as a way of life, and most would be sad at its parting. Most would look back with nostalgia and affection to the Training Ship that developed from the ashes of an ignominious broken backed HMS *Nile*. None would forget the two years that were to follow, as they were transformed from gawky self-conscious first term 'New Chums' into self-assured 'Quarter Boys' or QBs. None who joined the Old Boys' Association realised (how could they?) that they were joining an Association that would peak in the 60s, and thereafter suffer depletion by natural attrition. 'Quit ye like men, be strong!'

Life goes on, but no longer does a bugle sound 'reveille' to sleeping Cadets or the last lingering note of 'Last Post' sound over the Menai Strait – or the Thames – or the Solent – except, of course, in memory, and that must inevitably fade as the sun goes down.

CHAPTER 4

First Term

As so-called 'NEW CHUMS', the first few days were to take on a dreamlike quality as the settling-in process was begun into *Conway's* naval environment. Terminology and slang completely alien to most newcomers was bandied about routinely, and relative values had to be carefully reviewed. The most immediate threat seemed to come not from the Executive but rather from the Quarter Boys, or QBs so called, the Sixth Formers in normal collegiate terms, who by dint of their two-year seniority were about to satisfy the Board of Trade (then so called) that they had achieved a quarter of remission from four years' sea-going apprenticeship prior to professional examination. Quarter Boys. Simple really but a potentially dangerous breed, the majority of whom appeared to hold a profound amazement that anyone would wish to be a New Chum! This profundity often manifested itself (other than from the relatively few Cadet Captains) in demand that the newly arrived should sing, or otherwise demean themselves, before a QB group, and have their newly acquired uniform (favourite time was before Sunday Divisions) vaguely vandalised. Child-like in the event, scary at the time, but amusing in retrospect. Worst of the QBs were the well named 'shags', who by tacit acceptance had failed to contribute very much during their two years, other than a recognised contribution to the sales of cigarette manufacturers, and an extraordinary distortion of their uniform caps! They were aggressive towards slightly-built New Chums, but, hyena-like, group-laughingly withdrawn from obvious aspirants to the First XV front row!

Reception

The House Block, residence to all New Chums, was the unquestioned domain and responsibility of Chief Officer G. Drake, a fiercely grey-bearded father figure who ruled with strictness but with a keen eye for fair-play and naval discipline that largely contributed to the ability of most to come to terms with the strange new life and not uncommon pangs of homesickness. To this, the class of Autumn '53 was transported, rather oblivious to the beauty of Plas Newydd, and over-awed by the displayed self-confidence of the Cadet Captain made responsible for intake reception.

The front door of the House Block (actually a back door to the totality of the Marquis' residence, but front to *Conway*'s) took on the enormous responsibility of being 'the Gangway', but more was to come. Accustomed to the more normal division of pupils into 'houses', allocation of Cadets to 'Divisions' was readily understand-able, albeit that terminology was at first obscure – Mizzen, Main, Forecastle, Foretop and Hold, all heartily nautical and no doubt identifiable with the ship that spawned the shorebase.

To the left of the Gangway, past the Galley and up seven steps lay the Messdeck, and hereto the group was directed to muster for eventual dispersal through the accommodation. Corridors mysteri-ously became Alleyways, walls Bulkheads, ceilings Deckheads, whilst the floors of the building became Decks joined not by stairs but rather Companionways. Toilets were referred to as 'Heads' (which to the then uninitiated seemed a vertically reversed misnomer), whilst the domain of the Matron was 'Sick-bay'. A whirl of new information to be assimilated, or 'taken on board' to maintain the spirit of the thing, and bewildering not a little.

Each Division was divided into dormitories spread over two floors (decks), and each dormitory was named after merchant ships that had gained fame or recognition of one sort or another. '*Rawalpindi*', '*Andes*', '*Orontes*', '*Nestor*' and so forth. The dormitories themselves contained ranks of double-tiered bunks, and rather than wardrobes, accommodation for personal belongings and uniform attire was in 'lockers'. Most confusing to the New Chum was a small floor area in each dormitory, usually contained between two banks of lockers, known as 'Holy Ground', upon which Chums were forbidden to tread, other than in the pursuit of applying yet another coat of polish, or Ronuk, a trade-name to bring back to past Conways an overwhelming sense of nostalgic nausea! To the New Chum this extraordinary territorial arrogance was an initial nightmare. To tread across it inadvertently, in perambulating innocence, to achieve the shortest distance between two points (surely a navigational plus point) was to bring forth shocked explanation from more senior, and by then predatory, Cadets (old timers in their second term with many still wearing their falsetto), and, unbelievably, punishment! First transgression was reluctantly excusable, but the next became unfriendly.

'CHUM!' Forceful falsetto.

'Er, yes.' Recognition of status, still reluctant.

'You just walked across Holy Ground.' Smugly satisfied.

'Ah, right. No harm done, really. Really?'

'That's a club for you.'

'Er, what is a club?'

Receipt of a 'club', so-called, in dormitory terms, transpired to be the placing of one's upper arm muscle against the nearest locker corner, upon which the so placed member would receive a somewhat painful blow from the clenched fist of the current source of danger. Nothing nautical here, all good down to earth schoolboy tradition. Yet again, the more obvious aspirants to the First XV trod Holy Ground with relative impunity, their very size becoming overbearing bass to frustrated falsetto.

Cadet Captains were a more official threat, because they carried the badge of authority, vested in them by the Captain Superintendent and his officers. And the teaser! Justice sometimes, only sometimes, ringed with a very faint, yet tangible hint of sadism. The House boasted the presence of the Deputy Chief Cadet Captain, and a Junior Cadet Captain for each Division. Each had a teaser! Each new Cadet would, by some small, perceived misdemeanour, feel its caress, and thereafter seek to avoid it.

By way of explanation, the teaser was a length of rope (the rope's end, remember?) back spliced some six inches from its extreme end, and whipped. It was the nautical equivalent of the cane, and laid about the buttocks of an offending Cadet in quasi-ceremonial indignity, at least to the recipient! The sometimes alternative of standing to attention with a pillow on each hand of outstretched arms seemed at first attractive, until screaming biceps volunteered buttocks in Judas surrender!

The first morning 'reveille' call, after the brain-numbing first day of arrival, would be a ghastly screech of the Boatswain's Call over the Tannoy system, a hurried tumble from the unaccustomed top bunk to frantic appraisal of what piece of uniform went with what piece of uniform, and undignified jostle through the washrooms. Perhaps not that day, but on later days, would come the persuasive tones of the Duty Officer, as he intoned the time-honoured words: 'Wakey, wakey, rise and shine, the morning's fine, hands off cocks, and on socks!' Or, on that never to be forgotten morning, the hardly dulcet tones of Chief Officer Drake singing (yes singing!), 'Lazybones, lying in the sun, time to get the day's work done.' Wide-eyed, and unbelieving, the House Cadets responded!

First breakfast on the Mess-deck threw further confusion into the already hard-pressed New Chums (schooled no doubt in homely good manners and versed in comfortably domestic terminology) as local vernacular and custom burst about their ears. Grace solemnly spoken, an alarming set of demands.

'Chum, pass the soddock.' Unbelievably, this meant bread.

'Er, beg pardon, the what?'

'The soddock, and whilst you're at it, the grease.'

Mind galloping apace, this was reasonably identifiable as butter, and the next demand for 'spread' as marmalade or jam. No room for complacency, however, as the demand would out to pass the 'skilly'!

'Sorry, the what?'

'The tea, you nit-wit, the skilly.'

Served in large metal teapots, this brew was reputed to be heavily laced with bromide, and in total absence of homosexuality at Conway, who can doubt that as a truth! Perhaps Gweneth and Blodwyn, across the Straits, often pondered their lack of fulfilment – they would have been better served by Earl Grey, rather than temporary guests of the Marquis!

To those unaccustomed to institutional cooking, breakfast was an eye-opener, if not a bowel opener, comprising many baked beans, seemingly plastic fried eggs, and the ubiquitous Palethorpe sausage. Other meals, lovingly prepared by cooks apparently flung to the beach by their fellow sailors in sheer disgust, largely guaranteed to persuade all to write impassioned pleas to distant parents to upgrade the supply of tuck parcels.

The Conway Grace is paraphrased thus:

'We thank thee Lord for what we've had, it wasn't good, it wasn't bad, the meat was off, the skilly green, we thank thee Lord the plates were clean.'

(Purists of the Conway Grace will doubtless protest any poetic licence and inaccuracy here, but the sentiment is about right!)

The first Evening Rounds. These were the 'stand by your bunk time' as the Duty Officer toured the dormitories prior to lights out, for all the world like a hospital consultant, with his entourage of Cadet Captains acting as attendant housemen. There were teasers rather than stethoscopes, and they looked not at all undignified in their pyjamas, surmounted by uniform jacket and cap.

'ROUNDS'! Sharp shrill of the Boatswain's Call, and twinge of apprehension. Will authority frown upon you, or your little world of bunk and locker? Rigidly to attention, as only one day of naval discipline can teach you, and painfully unaware of possible pitfalls. The Duty Officer is magnanimous in his experience, and moves on – the Cadet Captains less so, and hover.

'Your locker is not ship-shape.'

'Oh, really? It looks, well, sort of all right to me.'

'Any further insolence from you, and you'll be in the washrooms.'

The situation would become alarming for reasons unknown, and safety sought in silence, a chance to evaluate how one should best turn this wooden wardrobe (locker) into something resembling the shape of a ship.

'Shake it up, and get it ship-shape, and less of the dumb insolence.' A trace of petulance here.

'Dumb insolence? What's that?'

'Don't get nervy with me, chum! Report to the washroom after Rounds.'

The entourage would depart, and the luckless Cadet would be surrounded by his fellows, all fraternal in their relief that another had taken the fire, and those of more seniority (almost everyone) effusive in their advice and guidance. Departure then from the dormitory with uniform trousers pulled over pyjamas, and accompanied by whispered support and encouragement from fellow-Cadets, and advice from 'old hands'.

'Keep your buttocks loose, don't tense up,' from one.

'As he swings the rope, stand up at the same time,' from a second.

'Shake his hand for God's sake, he's a bastard!' from a third.

Without knowledge of what was to come, all advice would be confusing, but to join the usual short queue of fellow-miscreants outside the washroom would be shortly thereafter to experience awareness of this new and painful experience.

The washroom, alarmingly filled with Cadet Captains, was always bright lit, and always pristine clean, each washbasin gleaming white.

'You will receive one cut,' the Deputy Chief Cadet Captain would intone, 'after which you will shake the hand of the Cadet Captain that administers it. Bend over that wash basin.'

Not all would seem to be right within the generally accepted scheme of things, and worth a question.

'What happens if I don't wish to shake his hand afterwards?' Good question, well reasoned.

'In that case,' would reply the Cadet Captain, 'I give you another cut!'

Forebrain reasons that this tax on tax system demands a bow to the inevitable, the wash basin and a tight lipped handshake after the stunning invasion of the buttocks by the teaser, followed by shuffled return to the dormitory. Tears would be restrained by pretension to manhood, and the final indignity:

'Show your bum, Chum. If he's drawn blood, you can report him!'

First homesickness, a very tangible thing, encouraged by distance, change, demands, Palethorpe's awful sausages, and the night mutters and noises of a roomful of sleeping Cadets. Not to mention the smarting weal raised neatly across the backside!

'Quit ye like men, be strong!'

Scholastic induction

The first term also introduced the New Chums into the Ship's Scholastic and Executive system, and whereas all were viewed as initial equals in the latter, new intakes were divided into Upper and Lower scholastic streams, placement no doubt influenced by results of entrance examinations and previous school reports. This was never defined, but certainly the first casting of the players was not necessarily finite, as achievement during these first months would sometimes see appropriate shuffling during the second term. Subjects of study took a familiar base, encompassing (no pun intended) Mathematics, Physics, English, History, Geography and for the odd few, Spanish, whilst nautical topping to the overall cake comprised Navigation and Chartwork, Ship Construction, Basic Engineering,

Meteorology, Seamanship and Signals. Ironically, some Cadets in that class of '53 held Mathematics and Physics as their most vulnerable subjects, and found that grappling with spherical trigonometry and that accursed man Archimedes and all his works was to become a Herculean task, extending far beyond *Conway's* exams to later professional Certificates of Competence, or 'tickets', so called. That the Science master, dedicated to all that he set about, really cared how much water would support a box-shaped vessel, or how many taps would fill that dreaded bath, remains a source of wonderment, but care he appeared to do, to the exclusion of all doubts on the part of his young charges. *Per ardua ad astra*, or thereabouts, and free surface effect eventually came alive, as did all things relatively unstable. Most Cadets in the Upper, and indeed Lower Stream appeared to have no such mental constraints, the learning of these new mysteries seemingly as natural as bodily functions, and the passing of exams equally as routine. Mercator's miracle of projection was by them assimilated with only momentary pause, rhumb and position lines perceived and plotted, sines halved and reversed with apparent ease, and the triangle spherical reduced to terrestrial simplicity with almost careless disdain.

The Headmaster was short, precise and with the rather unusual habit of placing the forefinger-tips of cathedralled hands into his nostrils, when puzzled or particularly contemplative. This structural symmetry was maintained by the thumb-pads placed lightly under the chin. His eyes usually twinkled, or reflected a deep concern to help one of his pupils over a problem hurdle. With often lengthy pauses between quick rushes of information or question, he was in essence a balance to executive authority, his well-worn mortarboard in counterpoint to the gold-braided cap of the Captain Superintendent.

'Is it possible to be moved to the Lower Stream, Sir? Finding it very difficult to keep up to class standard.'

Half term revelation, terrible self-doubt painfully surfaced, but dull relief in the asking. Pause for thought, and time to connect cathedralled fingers to waiting nostrils, head thrust forward from black-gowned shoulders. Eyes puzzled, but clearing to understanding and decision.

'No!' Stated with purpose and some impatience. 'You come here to experience hard work, and that is your commitment. Good luck, and request denied!'

Chinese philosophy will apply, with neither selectors nor players allowed to lose face.

'Quit ye like men, be strong!'

Simply stated, the task of the Headmaster and his tutorial team was, as in all nautical colleges, to sustain and develop basic schooling, while introducing their Cadet charges to those additional subjects so necessary to them in their merchant naval careers. This they did for the most part with delightful goodwill, no small degree of humour and considerable dedication. At the end of the two year scholastic road beckoned the *Conway* 'Extra' Certificate, coveted key in many cases to acceptance by shipping lines to their Indentures, and it was towards that goal that the staff directed their charges right from the start. (Interestingly, it was that Autumn Class of 1953 that was to be the first to sit the General Certificate of Education at *Conway*, a veritable landmark of progress in those days.) The *Conway* 'Extra' Certificate was widely recognised as the equivalent to University Matriculation and was awarded at the discretion of the Captain Superintendent to those who obtained 65% of examination, term and executive marks.

With the notable exceptions of gymnastics and boxing, presided over by the extraordinary agility of the Chief Petty Officer PTI, the school staff were also responsible for development of healthy minds and bodies through rugged application to sport. As at *Worcester* and Pangbourne, rugby ruled supreme, with membership of the First XV something akin to Masonry, with colours and caps the final apron. The Grand Master, of hoarse voice and considerable size, also taught physics, and took the nickname of Pug!

As Autumnal entrants, the new intakes were therefore prime potential devotees of the game, and no time was lost in the inculcation process. The red and white hooped jersey and white shorts became as important a part of uniform as the rest, the set pieces of the field almost as critically reviewed as Sunday Divisions. To say that there was an air of fanaticism about the game is probably to slightly understate the case, and the Honour of the Ship had to be defended annually in traditional matches with HMS *Worcester* and Pangbourne. Much transgression in other fields of endeavour would be impatiently shrugged aside in pursuit of that particular triple victory!

'Obvious weakness in the key subjects', whilst cause for no small concern, scarcely rated alongside the more important announcement that 'he has developed into a good three-quarter, and shows promise for the First XV before he leaves the Ship.'

Appraisal was very much a two-way affair in the first few weeks, as teacher and pupil weighed and concluded each to the other, and certainly it was affectionately concluded that *Conway* held its share of tutorial characters, so important to the successful mix of school environment. Few who joined the then History class will ever forget him who, by repute, had played chess with Rommel in the Western Desert, and who had become a rare exponent of 'the Club' when attention would momentarily wander from his dusting off of History. 'Don't be wet,' he would intone as salacious snigger greeted his description of India's Rajahs that 'chewed bang and fondled concubines'. 'Take a club,' he would roar, and the class would fall apart in great disarray! He took the nickname 'Humph'.

Memorable too was he who taught English, the 'Prune', who would in later terms develop the latent thespian ability in the Ship to produce extraordinary successful productions of *Journey's End* and *Morning Departure*, before fond parents. His class control was uniquely competent, and it was with obvious attention and taut-held interest that his charges would listen as he sat atop table or desk, black gown tightly wrapped round stooped shoulders and gangled legs, reading aloud whole stories of Somerset Maugham. His smile was rare, but his sense of humour real, if somewhat mischievous – how else to explain the whimsical retention within an otherwise carefully censored script of *Morning Departure* the thoughtful words of a bottomed submariner – 'mounted over the gate, my Coat of Arms will be a pair of women's legs, fat and rampant.' Heady stuff, that, in the early 50s!

By sheer bounce, enthusiasm and seemingly unbounded energy, he who taught Science that first term held his class to their tasks, and later scattered them like chaff as he hurled his tracksuited bulk among them on the rugby pitch, either in training or as a grim determined opponent in the staff seven-a-side team! Never still, always involved and whilst his nickname was perhaps unkind and hardly descriptive, he was affectionately referred to as the 'Sporting Arse'.

Balanced somewhere between scholastic and executive, the Ship's Chaplain or Padre reserved unto himself a position of considerable importance and influence not only for his spiritual guidance, but perhaps more mundanely for reason that he exercised control over dispensing of pocket-money. Secondly, he had a nose that could detect cigarette smoke or residual fumes over a considerable distance! Issue of pocket-money was a time that stretched patience to the screaming limit as he insisted on making his ledger entries in slow, painstaking copper-plate writing, a ceremony that each recipient had to attend to its drawn-out conclusion; whilst a sniff and searching glance in the direction of a smoker would mean sure detection, albeit rare reportage, and a feeling of considerable insecurity in the offender for days. Distinctive too in his white-hooded tracksuit as he maintained the training that had made him a marathon runner. One could perhaps ignore his Church, but never its Champion!

Pre-sea Training College it was, however, and in unquestioned command was the Captain Superintendent, full four-ringed Captain, Royal Naval Reserve, more distanced by his braid and ultimate authority. To his officers fell the responsibility for the executive side of the establishment and the moulding of a motley arrival of New Chums into a homogeneous group responsive to the naval traditions and disciplines that prevailed; moreover, to instil into them more than a nodding acquaintance with practical seamanship, power, pulling and sailing craft, and all matters nautical relevant to the chosen career of those that passed through their hands. Variously uniformed as Lieutenant-Commanders or Lieutenants Royal Naval Reserve, Merchant Navy officers (usually on secondment) or with the distinctive badges and braid of HMS *Conway* itself, they went about their business with authority and purpose, a lot of understanding, and like their gown-clad school counterparts, no small degree of good humour. Theirs was to apply yardsticks of achievement previously unheard of by those new Cadets – ZEST, DISCIPLINE and BEARING, whilst later terms would see critiques levelled at ABILITY IN POWER, PULLING AND SAILING BOATS, together with RELIABILITY, POWER OF COMMAND, and SENSE OF RESPONSIBILITY.

'The marks given for executive subjects must not be interpreted in the same way as these for academic subjects. The qualities commented on herein can only be judged relative to other Cadets in the same Top and if ALL boys in a Top are of a high standard any individual Cadet's marks will appear average, similarly if ALL boys in the Top are below standard, the marks will still appear average. Divisional Officers comments must therefore be studied as well as the marks awarded.'

Executive induction

Everything 'executive' was at first alien and strange, beginning with the grouping of Cadets into Divisions, thence to the Royal Navy two-watch system of port and starboard, and further sub-divided into 'first-part' and 'second-part'. Allocation of cleaning duties referred to 'parts of ship', and daily routines and organisation drew largely upon those practised by the Royal Navy in their Harbour or Sea Routines. The nautical effect was further heightened and emphasised in the House by the Tannoy system, strangely akin to that employed afloat, with each routine order or information of general interest being preceded by the No. 12 pipe on the Boatswain's Call, and usually the words 'D'ye hear there!', and followed by the perfunctory 'Carry on'.

'Cooks to the galley.'

'Duty Watch, muster on the gangway!'

'Hands to clean part of ship, stand fast cooks and sweepers.'

'Hands to clean.'

'Hands to breakfast.'

'Out pipes – duty watch to muster.'

'Hands to school.'

And so it proceeded, at usually a devilish pace, lacking only wind and wave for final effect.

'Hands to clean into the rig of the day.' Combinations of uniform clothing to be remembered and adhered to, all at first confusingly referred to by numbers No. 1s, No. 2s, No. 5s, No. 8s and so forth, and why on earth does one 'clean' into another suit of clothing? The Executive Officers, constrained by uniform and the need to display and teach the appropriate discipline, were less able to be seen as 'characters', but despite themselves, they emerged and were labelled as such – most notably the two Chief Officers, one in charge of the 'House', and the other, the more senior, responsible for the 'Camp'. The former was gruff, bearded and avuncular, very much a Merchant Navy Officer and so uniformed. The latter was thin lipped and purple handed in the cold, thoughtful and determined behind his wire-rimmed glasses, a Lieutenant-Commander, Royal Naval Reserve, late of the Merchant Service, called Brook-Smith. Each in his own way gained the respect of the Cadets that they trained, but no more so than in that first impactive term, when men had to be sorted from boys and family replaced by surrogates.

Not forgetting, of course, the Chief Petty Officer PTI who doubled as ship's barber. His 'cabin' in the House harboured the new-fangled electric haircutters that reduced proud hair to pudding basin style, always preceded by that well recognised cry of the Hairdressers' Guild: 'Next victim please!' Skinner by name, and by nature in that role.

Introduction to the intricacies of parade-training brought moments of hilarity or despair and a wealth of new meaning to the phrase 'two left feet'. Most amusing to those not so afflicted was the sight of others with a left arm that was apparently committed to sympathetic unison movement with the left leg, right arm with right leg – camel marching, so called. Shambles ensued as individuals struggled to become a squad, wheeling, turning, about turning, halting (wrong footed again), dressing to the left or right (a tailoring term?) and generally seeking symmetry. How, when and who to salute, eyes right, eyes left, eyes in the back of your head. Double march, slow marches, all by the left or right but always off on the left foot. The left foot, you idiot! Some Cadets had attended previous schools as members of the Army Cadet Corps, and now had to resist the stamping foot of the pongo (naval definition, 'small brown animal of limited intelligence') and the salute that took the longest way up and the longest way down. The grounds of Plas Newyd played host to all this activity, and the Chums as newcomers played to a derisive audience of experienced accomplishment, soon to become theirs by sheer necessity. 'New hands' would become 'Old hands', able to march to the sometimes doubtful beat of the band, that erstwhile group of drummers and buglers who practised behind the cricket pavilion, providing from its number appropriate pomp at Sunday Divisions, Reveille and Last Post. No-one who experienced it would forget that first march at double pace from the Dock, from water's edge back up the steep road through rhododendrons whose beauty was lost to the exhausted eyes of the passing squad, heavy with their battledress, sea-boots and oilskins and filthy from their first endeavours at wire splicing, buoy laying and general messing about in boats under the jaundiced eye of the Boatswain. They would quit themselves like men, and superficially, at least, display strength! Notwithstanding, and as in all things, reward came through accomplishment and learning, recognition through achievement, and whilst the 'Big Bertha' oar of the clumsy Cutters could never become a friend, or the more sophisticated needs of the Gigs an ally, their demands of usage were slowly but surely brought into perspective, and overcome. Drill became commonplace, and the wearing of Her Majesty's uniform, in all its forms, routine. After all, rejecting the system was to reject all those hours of family scheming – joining it was to succeed in the endeavour! Most chose to join, that first term.

Canteen

Relatively safe haven for the 'New Chum' was the canteen, although relative in the sense that it lay within the heart of the Camp, residence of those much-feared Senior Cadets. It needed therefore to be carefully negotiated prior to enjoying its delights, a break from normal 'ship's' food. Walls, brown tiled from floor for some two feet, were surmounted by green tile capping, for all the world like a Victorian lavatory but with the saving grace of a wood-trestle supported ceiling. Unashamedly authoritarian to his wife behind the scenes in the kitchen, but always sympathetic to his young customers, the Welsh canteen manager would hear the anxious enquiring order for sustenance, and in roaring tone transmit it with startling noise to the kitchen behind.

'One beans on toast, one cup of cawfee – and make it snappy, woman!'

More bittersweet than the friendliness of the canteen was the arrival of LETTERS FROM HOME, that first term. There was painful readjustment to news of loved ones; and the awful recognition that newly-found independence was only a thin veneer so easily scratched by words of love and crosses representative of kisses. There was never time to loiter or look for self-pity, however.

'OUT PIPES, DUTY WATCH TO MUSTER ON THE GANGWAY!!!'

Home leave

Home-coming from that first term was to all 'New Chums' an event
not to be forgotten in its importance. Sloughed forever from their
shoulders was the hated reference to their newness, and three months
had bestowed a familiarity with uniform and disciplined posture that
in most would be immediately recognised and applauded by
anxiously awaiting parents and friends. Crewe Station saw the
unexpected event of one *Conway* Cadet being saluted by a Royal
Naval Rating, the salute being formally acknowledged without
second thought or qualm. Well, almost so, and only a momentary
feeling of panic!

The Eastbourne Corporation bus conductor had a puzzled look
about him, en route from Old Town to the Winter Gardens that first
leave. Emboldened to escort the much-cherished daughter of
neighbours to a dance, the self-assured and uniformed escort to the
formally attired young lady solemnly and importantly proffered the
fare.

'One and a half to the Winter Garden, please.'

'And who, may I ask, is the half?' came the question. So was pomp
so quickly deflated by circumstance!

CHAPTER 5

Third and Fifth Terms

AFTER TWO TERMS AT THE HOUSE, two-year entry Cadets were viewed as sufficiently prepared for the move to a higher plane of existence, and in the past, that would have meant to the Ship. No longer so, however, as the Camp, spawned at the death throes, awaited their coming with some anticipation. They were no longer Chums but having assumed a certain gossamer thin mantle of seniority within the confines of incubator House, were to discover that the sense of security into which they had been temporarily lulled was a transient thing. The few rungs of ladder climbed merely led to the bottom of yet another! How short lived the feeling of superiority bestowed by the simple knowledge that Holy Ground between the dormitory lockers could be stepped upon with impunity, and that punitive 'ronuking' was Chums' fate. (Not many dictionaries, if any, recognise the verb 'to ronuk', irregular in brief declension with 'you ronuk', or 'you will ronuk' (present indicative) echoed only by the past participle 'I have ronuked'. A common noun also glossed over by Oxford and others is 'ronuker', often adjectively referred to as 'that (or the) bloody ronuker', a weighted polishing instrument with a long handle, training and practice in the use of which was part of *Conway*'s long tradition.) At the Camp, third termers ronuked!

The Camp was, as its name implies, initially emergency canvas pitched after loss of the Ship, thereafter replaced by battlegrey, long wooden huts, grouped neatly to the right of the entrance to the grounds of Plas Newydd, for all the world like some wartime Stalag Luft slipped quietly into the Welsh countryside. Each Division was allocated two such huts (one port watch, one starboard) and each accommodated some twenty Cadets with a Cadet Captain. Within each Division's hut resided the Senior Cadet Captain for the Division, always a QB (sixth termer) with authority recognised by residence of his own cabin. Division Huts formed the east and west perimeters of the Camp square, and were separated by several hundred feet of carefully tended grass with paved pathways inscribing

27

a Cross of St George across the green heartland. To the south of the rectangle was the Mess Hut, whilst to the north the only permanent building of the group, the canteen, rubbed shoulders with cabined accommodation of officers and teaching staff who 'lived in'. This Camp, this offspring of the Ship's demise, was umbilically connected to the House Block by the roadway that swept south to the School Block and thence westered less sedately down to the placenta from which originated nourishment, the galley or kitchens. No trivial analogy this for from the House kitchens little blue vans would take their loads of insulated containers each and every mealtime to the Camp mess-deck, there to be unloaded by the drivers always recognisable by their blue food-stained trousers and rarely white, equally stained, shirts and loud Liverpool profanities!

It is probably fair to say that the ubiquitous Palethorpe sausage travelled not necessarily well, whilst the plastic eggs of breakfast gently congealed that little while longer. Cornflakes were in much demand, resistant in the main to such logistical travails! On par, the House Cadets probably fared better than their more senior counter-parts, being closer to source supply. A very relative judgement, nonetheless.

To this then, that Summer term of '54, came the Cadets from the House. Their new quarters, those long grey huts, entered past one single closeted lavatory and oil-skin locker, contained two serried rows of metal-framed beds. Each bed was adjacent not to a locker, but to a sea-chest, a wooden cabin trunk style of clothing accommo-dation that would have brought tears of acclamation to the eyes of long-departed square-rig sailors or steerage passengers, but were pitiless in their new demands upon Cadets from the House, now accustomed to more utilitarian stand-up lockers. Beds were allocated on a seniority basis, the most junior closest to the entrance, staggered upward towards the far end of the hut where resided the Junior Cadet Captain and the fire-escape door. This arrangement was of no great significance, other than to underline a school need somehow to demonstrate some form of superiority in an environment that otherwise reduced all to a mundane sameness. It also provided a nocturnal unobtrusive exit for the smokers!

Washing facilities, so comfortably available in the House, were here non-existent. The limb-jerking, sleep dispelling raucous notes of the Reveille bugle, yet another mark of progress away from the House, heralded the birth of tousled activity as half-clad Cadets tumbled from their huts, washbags and towels at the trail, to double in mostly dispirited style down the road to the school block, there to ablute, regardless of bitter cold or pouring rain.

The more thought provoking and sinister side of the House washrooms, the after-rounds appointment with teaser-wielding Cadet Captains, was absent from the Camp, but this gave rise to no grounds for complacency. Here the Senior Cadet Captains had their own common room for such punitive excursions (the Gun Room, so called), and they seemed much more adept and practised in the application. Life, overall, became no easier!

This was, however, the summer term, and whilst the senior rugby master fretted and pined the warm months away, other activities were undertaken with enthusiasm by all others. The waters of the Menai Strait came alive with gigs and cutters, sail boats and indeed swimmers, as the cross-Strait annual swimming race took place, invariably through a mass of white jelly-fish that appeared to arrive to the Strait for the event. Skills so damply gained during previous months were practised and put to a final test during the round-Puffin Island sailboat race, whilst stroke and big bertha oars seemed less hostile as they dipped and flashed in bright sunlight. Blue shorts became rig of the day, albeit somewhat incongruously topped by blue shirts and white stiff collars, and the main rugby pitch, denuded of its white goalposts, took upon its greensward the white lines of athletics track, and cricket square. The Master of History, one time chess challenger to Rommel in the Western Desert, twitched his moustache like a true and eager Desert Rat and took upon himself the challenge of forming a presentable cricket squad, whilst he that taught English coaxed and cajoled his would-be Thespians towards the Parents' Day theatrical presentation.

Llanedwan Parish Church saw its Sunday delivery of worshipping Cadets arrive at its ancient gates by marching squad, having swung comfortably along the one and a half miles of sun-dappled country road that separated it from Plas Newydd, the Cadets' white-topped uniform caps bearing further testimony to summer's presence. The Mermaid Inn at Foel, a mere 4 ½ miles from Plas Newydd, beckoned invitingly to staff parched after long summer days of pressured

activity, and gave welcome relief in its timbered haven, satisfyingly
and totally inaccessible to Cadets!

To the Third Termer, this summer term was almost the slack water
that lay between the turn of tides, but for the QB or sixth former, it
was the high water of his time at *Conway*, marked thus by final
examinations, acceptance by the shipping line of his choice, passing
out parade and final departure. It was, most notably, the one term of
each year that the Queen's Gold Medal was presented to one of a
group of five Cadets, invariably QBs, short-listed by the Captain
Superintendent with the final choice by decree being left to the
personal votes of all Cadets training in the Ship at that time. It is
probably germane to observe that Senior Cadet Captains with hopes
for eligibility became far more circumspect in the use of the teaser
during these summer months, or was it that justice became tempered
by preoccupation with upcoming finals?

Water was not totally slack, however, for the Autumn entrants of
1953 were to become the first Cadets to sit the General Certificate
of Education from *Conway*, and it was during this third term that the
deed had to be done, the Oxford and Cambridge School Examination Board requiring to be suitably satisfied and impressed by papers
written in, as one recalls, the gymnasium. Suffice it to say that those
Cadets roundly satisfied the Board, and in consequence the Headmaster and his staff, who had no doubt awaited the results in some
fear.

'Merit-half', the one half day of each term when Cadets were
allowed off the grounds of Plas Newydd into the local economy, was
theoretically made more pleasant in the summer, the trek into Bangor
by Crossville Bus, or perhaps walk to Llanfair PG or Menai Bridge,
less hostile than under the thunderous skies and lashing rain of the
winter months. That the local economy took more kindly to the brief
release is open to some doubt, but somehow the weather could
encourage a smile to the face of the usually inhibited North Welsh,
or even an occasional word in English, rather than their native
tongue. Except of course, when it rained.

That particular term it rained on 'merit-half' day, and those that
had avoided the imposition of a 'demerit', awarded either scholasti-
cally or executively, shrugged reluctantly into blue uniform raincoats

and prepared themselves for a few hours of freedom as best could be achieved. A few had the rare good fortune of parental or family visitors, even though officially discouraged, and theirs was generally the better half-day save for the fond farewells in the evening. That it was also a Sunday that term posed further potential constraints upon activities. Unaware of, or perhaps disbelieving in, local Sunday customs, the Royal Naval Commander who had collected his son and one other Cadet drove forth from Plas Newydd gates and in the general direction of Holyhead, to an hotel. His astonishment was real when informed that alcoholic drinks were unavailable on the Sabbath, but undeterred ordered a swift return to the car park where he triumphantly flung open the boot of his vehicle to announce that iron-rations would be issued immediately. The bottles of beer, resident therein, thus fulfilled the purpose for which he had thoughtfully provided them. Forbidden fruit by any local standard this, and did the Padre's nose twitch just briefly back at the ship?

The third term came to an inevitable close. Parents were suitably enthralled by *Journey's End*, Douglas V. Duff as Visiting Dignitary and Old Conway made his awesomely boring speech in the summer marquee, Ship's Company was adequately paraded, and prizes presented. The Boatswain looked thoughtfully at the line of mooring buoys in the Menai Strait that would need to be retrieved next term through the salt and oil-stained efforts of Cadets balanced precariously and wetly on the fore-deck of the Pinnace, whilst the senior rugby master looked at the autumn with thinly veiled anticipation, his hibernation at a near close. The Desert Rat looked sadly at the cricket square but, ever positive, twitched his moustache towards next summer.

Plas Newydd once more fell silent as her Conways decamped for homes, and the Marquis came out to play.

Fifth term

The Fourth Term of Autumn 1954 thrust its way through the autumnal months fired not only by the ever present demands of scholastic, executive and rugby life ('keen tackler and faller on the ball'), but spiced too by the knowledge that Christmas was approaching. This meant the possibility of a special present to some fortunates among the original Autumn term of 1953. It was not the 'plain unmarked' package that arrived for one unfortunate Cadet, loudly announced by the Mail Cadet Captain on the breakfast mess-deck, containing female hygiene products and ordered whimsically on his behalf. Nor indeed was it a formal response from the French Foreign Legion (equally whimsical enquiry placed on his behalf) that advised the self-same Cadet to apply in person to their Paris Headquarters, having made his own way thereto! It was the possibility of being promoted from Cadet to Junior Cadet Captain, from schoolboy to prefect, although the analogy with normal school scarcely bore comparison to its Naval College importance.

Several were informed that they were to wear the coveted gold insignia on the left lower uniform sleeve, and arrived home at term end to, all so casually, display the prize hastily stitched on uniform jackets for the journey back from *Conway*.

The Fifth Term therefore held a special poignancy for some, as those that theretofore had travelled as a group had now to re-evaluate their positions one relative to the other in the executive field, whilst overall there was an added fever to the pace in the knowledge that the next term was the last, and much had to be achieved meantime. Time was running out, and decisions had to be made as to which Shipping Line to apply to for future apprenticeship, with work to be done to achieve the means of persuading the Line of choice that the applicant (supplicant?) was of acceptable standard.

Humour, notwithstanding, continued to flavour the mix, and whilst close attention was paid to him that now taught Navigation to that Fifth Term, his quasi-American accent perpetuated to his new charges the long standing nickname of the 'Sheriff of Deadwood.' He would rarely leave his class without a cardboard star affixed to the back of his black, chalk dusted gown, having routinely awarded a good part of the class with 'a whole half demerit', pronounced with close to a Bostonian clip. To ignore the Liverpudlian Cadet who rose occasionally from behind his desk-lid with stockinged face and the words 'stick 'em up' was to demonstrate masterly Class Authority, and the expected 'take a half demerit' gained only perfunctory pause from the rush of knowledge that he had to impart.

The senior Maths Master too, interesting and brilliant in his then knowledge of computers, was easily diverted from the agonies of differentiating the area beneath a curve. He continued to give lip service to the common belief that an orchestrated and muted hum from assembled Cadets would cause him to think that his hearing aid was playing up. Twinkle eyed beneath his iron grey crew cut, he would make the pretence adjustment to the offending ear-piece, and honour would be roundly satisfied, respect maintained. Some curves, too, were finally differentiated!

The historians had an unexpected term sabbatical from the Desert Rat, and history became dull in consequence. The teaching of English, perhaps as result of a surfeit of Somerset Maugham, fell to the Ship's Padre, and was cloistered in consequence. Fifth Term locums perhaps allowed the usual practitioners to gather strength for the final Sixth Term burst that was to come!

As to Science which was, ominously, to become Applied Science in the Sixth Term, he who was senior rugby master took charge, and was rather gruffly humourless in his dedication towards the teaching of his subject. He was as uncompromising as toward his First XV Squad in training and play.

The Captain Superintendent, aloof in his position and four ringed authority, with his green Rover that whisked him between House and Office on the Camp Quarterdeck, continued to give little clue as to his opinions on the progress of individual Cadets, demanding only that standards of discipline and training remained high, with the well-being of the whole Ship his total concern. That he would acknowledge his Fifth Term Cadets sometimes now by name was not always adjudged as necessarily good, but certainly it was conceded that his watchful eye missed little and that any sign of fifth term faltering would be noted and headed off. If anything, and because of penultimate term status, it was a greater danger zone.

The Chief Officer of the Camp, Lieutenant Commander RNR and Divisional Officer from the Mizzen Top Division, asserted his authority evenhandedly, displaying only slight bias toward his own Division, and doggedly pursued all towards excellence. For all their importance in the scheme of things, however, the Executive Staff somehow now took second place to the demands of school achievement.

Choice of Shipping Company was now of paramount importance, and where before Training Ship brochures had been closely examined

and evaluated, now the offered opportunities of a myriad of Lines,
then available but now largely demised, were studied and discussed.
Their demands of achievement were weighed against scholastic and
executive reports on progress to date in the knowledge that there was
only one more term to go. Applications were made, vetted for
authority by authority, and despatched to await the call for interview,
or rejection and re-application to second or third choice as the case
was to be. For one Cadet, it was a no-choice situation, in that he had
long decided that his future was destined to be with the Peninsular
& Oriental Steam Navigation Company, and no thought was given
to anything else, other than to seek appointment as Midshipman,
Royal Naval Reserve, meantime. Others saw their opportunities
elsewhere, and many arguments and discussions raged through the
grey huts as to why and wherefore, but overall it was the beginning
of waiting time, in many cases only to be finalised by sixth term
results and interviews.

CHAPTER 6

Sixth Term

THOSE AUTUMNAL CHUMS OF 1953 returned to Plas Newydd as Quarter Boys, having almost run their two year course. Some by now had been promoted to Senior Cadet Captains, one to Chief Cadet Captain, and one to Deputy Chief Cadet Captain. In this, nothing was different from those many terms of QBs that had preceded them.

Slotted into the more usual life of the Ship now came interviews with Shipping Lines, and for some, the Board for Midshipmen Royal Naval Reserve, that final attempt to juxtapose Royal to Merchant, to claw something back from the fact that Dartmouth had somehow been inaccessible those two years ago.

London was full of summer sunshine, and paid scant heed to those that made their unaccustomed and selfconscious way to Admiralty House to be interviewed by officers appointed by Their Lordships. For those with thoughts of the battleship grey efficiency of the Royal Navy and the pomp and circumstance that went with it, introduction to the means of movement between Admiralty House floors came as a sobering revelation. The dark, wood-lined lift was manned by an uniformed operator of indeterminate age and rating, one hand distinguished by the wearing of a leather pad. From ceiling to floor of the lift ran a rope and on hearing the floor required, this apparent exponent of marine campanology gave mighty heave upon the manila and up shot the cage at alarming pace. Judging his moment, and now demonstrating the need for the padded hand, his fist clamped upon the rope to bring the vehicle to a bobbing halt at its destination, and with total nonchalance he opened the cage doors.

'Your floor, Sir,' he rasped, and with a rattle of meshed metal doors and a heave at the rope, he disappeared downwards at speed towards lower floors, hopefully not to lose his pad en route, as that would spell disaster.

The Interview Board was generally coloured gold, at least by lasting impression, with lace of rank seemingly running forever in

repeated circles round the arms of the officers that comprised the
Board. The would-be Midshipman sat in lonely isolation on one side
of the table, and tried his best to answer responsibly the questions of
the opposing team, fielded in strength and ranged ominously on the
command, or other side, of the table. To this day the questions and
responses remain dreamlike in sequence and forgotten in context, only
the breathtaking return to the ground floor with that Quasimodo of
Admiralty House, and indeed the earlier ascent, remaining firmly fixed
in memory. How accustomed must he have become to the looks of
fascinated disbelief as he hauled his cage up and down the lift shaft of
Admiralty House, and how many nations had concluded to join war
against Britain faced with this demonstration of Her Majesty's Naval
sophistication. However, and for all that, Appointment Number 7206,
Probationary Midshipman Royal Naval Reserve was granted on
1 August 1955 and so recorded, together with other successful
candidates by the Registrar General of Shipping and Seamen in
Cardiff. Juxtaposition had been achieved, at least as a beginning.

That summer term ran its normal course, the QBs as always acutely
aware of their obvious importance and proximity to the actual
business of going to sea that now placed them firmly apart from their
fellow cadets. Small but significant milestones marked the way
through the term, not least of all the receiving of the dreaded 'jabs'
(TAB and cholera) so efficiently and matter of factly dispensed by the
resident sister at the sickbay, that little haven of quietness and smell
of ether (not ronuk!) disposed on the first floor of the House. Matron,
a Welsh dragon with a sharp tongue, a short fuse for malingerers and
a twinkle always lurking at the back of the eyes, presided here, ably
assisted by the Assistant Matron, younger, quiet toned but equally able
to take authoritative charge of an over enthusiastic cadet. The 'jab'
was usually requested by the recipient to be administered to the right
arm, thus exempting him on a temporary basis from the need to
salute masters and officers, visitors and Marquises. To demonstrate this
entitlement, a white marker was worn on the appropriate uniform
sleeve, mute witness to the pain being borne with such stoicism and
fortitude. Regrettably this selfsame marker appeared to act like a
magnet to iron filings, with a wealth of people wishing to prod at it
with a puzzled question as to its purpose, and a sudden rash of friends
all inexplicably wishing to slap the arm in friendly fashion. Walls and

locker doors, desk lids and doorjambs all conspired to leap upon the damaged member to hear that low Anglo-Saxon with nautical overtones that had also been learned these five terms past, albeit used with utmost discretion in fear of teasered reprimand!

Of much greater note, however, was the never to be forgotten occasion of the Captain's Dinner, that only occasion when the Captain Superintendent and his Lady extended hospitality to the Chief Cadet Captain, Deputy Chief Cadet Captain and the Senior Cadet Captain of each Division, to mark the high point of their final term at the Ship.

The normal rigidity of nervousness was helped not one little bit by the unaccustomed wing collar and bow tie that appeared to take away all normal movement of the head, reducing it to a stiff and formal lateral swivel, as the eyes sought direction for the mouth to respond to stilted dinner table conversation.

The Captain Superintendent was immaculate in full Mess Dress and his wife in formal gown to receive their guests in their quarters overlooking the Menai Strait, set aside for their use by the Marquis. There too was the fabled brass telescope, and one glance was enough to satisfy the accuracy of reports that little could escape overview by the Captain on the Strait. It was a dinner that stretched out as an agony of suspense for the cadets, placed for the first time in such close and intimate proximity to deity, and brought to a crescendo of apprehension by the insistence of the Captain's wife that dessert fruit should be eaten with knife and fork. Unfortunately this bombshell was dropped only after selection from the fruit bowl, and for those that had taken the grapes the embarrassment of skating the elusive damp green fruits onto the polished table surface became acute for the perpetrater, and the cause of muffled hysterical guffaws hastily swallowed by those more fortunate who had chosen the banana. That is, until confronted by the sight of the hostess deftly skinning her banana with appropriate cutlery, with the obvious expectation that others would follow her example. That the Captain and his Lady had both played out their game before was left in little doubt, and it served as a timely reminder that outwith the confines of the *Conway* mess-decks, there existed many social occasions that would call upon a little more sophistication than the rude demand for soddock and skilly, and a frenzied grab at beans and Palethorpe. It was an experience that thankfully came to its inevitable close, with relief finally loosening tongues as the cadets tumbled back into that part of the Marquis' residence allocated to the *Conway*, to be met by the disbelieving eyes of very junior cadets who scurried about on the never-ending ronuk duty, prior to evening rounds. Sudden realisation of rank, and readjustment to the relative scheme of things.

'Watch it, Chum!'

The Deputy Chief Cadet Captain, resident at the House and aware that the roof afforded unusual sanctuary to smokers determined or knowledgeable enough to know of the existence of the trapdoor leading thereto, concluded that in his final term he too would smoke a cigarette, secure in the knowledge that the house was deserted of both staff and Cadets, all attendant upon games activities of one sort or another. Repairing thus to the leaded parapets of the House, he spluttered over the ritual of lighting and smoking the forbidden plant, enjoying it not one little bit, and reluctant to admit the failure of this little expedition. Carefully extinguishing the remains, he slipped quickly back through the trapdoor, and casually descended to the second floor, quietly satisfied that his excursion was both undetected and undetectable in its solitary enterprise. A black gowned, dog-collared Padre twinkled past on fast moving little legs, his nose twitching and eyes knowing, appearing apparently from thin air and disappearing fast down the 'gangway' to the next 'deck'.

'Been having a quick smoke, have we?' he questioned as he brushed past, 'not good, not good!' and rushed back behind his looking glass, there no doubt to chuckle at the ghastly discomfiture left behind.

Final term it was, however, with all the frantic swotting for final examination in the *Conway* 'Extra' Certificate, preparation for the Parents' Open Day and Passing Out Parade and the realisation that two years of study, activity in matters nautical and sporting, and acquired comradeship were coming to an end. The last few Sunday afternoon letters home, the last tuck parcels received, and reluctantly the last haircut from the PTI to get safely through final Sunday Divisions. The last roaring rendition of the 'Conway Song', words now as routinely known as the Lord's Prayer at Church Parade, and the inevitable cross-referencing of friends' home addresses for future contact to be maintained which, just as inevitably, they were not.

'Subject to satisfactory results in final examinations, and successful completion of the Outward Bound School at Ullswater, the Peninsular and Oriental Steam Navigation Company will he pleased to offer Three Year Indenture to this Cadet as Apprentice to the Company', or words to that effect, was music to the ears of the applicant.

The term drew to a close, and presentation of *Morning Departure* was successfully played to an appreciative audience of parents, whilst on the sports field athletes demonstrated their acquired or natural skills in disciplined sequence.

The elements were appropriately kind that day in July 1955, and as the sun shone hotly upon the spacious grounds of the Marquis of Anglesey, so a cooling breeze blew in across the Menai Strait to bring some relief to the perspiringly uniformed Cadets of HMS *Conway*, wheeling sturdily in practised symmetry past the saluting dais, and not one Divisional Cadet Captain fluffed his 'eyes left' command as his Division passed the Captain Superintendent and visiting dignitary. On parade dispersal, recipients of prizes marched forward one by one to receive them from the hands of the visiting dignitary, Sir Donald Anderson, Chairman of the Shipping Federation and Deputy Chairman of the P & O Company: the Tate Prize, the Captain Price Prize, Awards of the Mercantile Marine Service Association, the Honourable Company of Master Mariners Prize, the Rankin Prize and the Laird Prize, and many more besides for achievement in all matters nautical, scholastic, technical and executive.

For one Cadet, the day held particular significance as he marched forward to receive the Queen's Gold Medal that he had been privileged to be awarded, to be presented by the very hands of the Deputy Chairman of the company into whose august Indenture he was to enter. Sir Donald, immaculate in his double-breasted grey suit and imposing in his distant looks and bushy eyebrows, accepted salute and offered his hand in congratulation to the tense cadet before him. 'Well done, well done, and what company do you intend to join!'

(As fate was to have it, Sir Donald and this cadet were to meet in another July, this time in 1961, the former now Chairman of' the P & O, the latter a Third Officer, the occasion the maiden voyage of the *Canberra*, the newly launched flagship of the P & O.)

This term had an unexpected twist in its tail however. As parents strove to load accumulated accoutrements to waiting cars, and farewells strayed longer into overtime, the Captain Superintendent moved to a disciplinary posture as befitted his position, and as was his unfortunate duty. Belatedly discovered, and no doubt too soon for one ill-disposed cadet, the vehicle of one of the officers was found to have sugar in its tank, and the Captain decreed that 'shore leave' would be delayed until such time as the miscreant confessed. Whether or not he did is to the writer unknown, but suffice it to say that all were mightily inconvenienced for some time thereafter, with parents suddenly thrust into the disciplinary environment so familiar to their offspring. To the very end, naval discipline was the code of the ship and was so observed and displayed. Be strong, quit ye like men, but quit not until 'liberty men ashore' is bugled.

Eventually away from the Ship for the last time, with admitted backward glances of some sadness, the cadet from Eastbourne drove away with family, for the last time through Llanfair PG, towards the Menai Bridge, Bangor and eventually the south. As befitted the moment, stop-off was made at a public house in the village of Menai Bridge, to take a celebratory stirrup cup or somesuch, with Grandfather as undisputed spokesman for the group. He ordered the appropriate beverages, to include a pint of bitter for his grandson, still so obviously uniformed as a cadet of *Conway*, and resident therefore within the tender age of seventeen years.

'Is he over eighteen?' queried the Welsh barmaid.

Grandfather struck an imposing figure. Flushed with the day's events, and never ready to be challenged, the answer came roaring out and brooked no further interference:

'Eighteen? – eighteen? – of course he's bloody eighteen, woman!'

'By permission of the Ministry of Transport the Holder of this Certificate (Conway Extra Certificate) is allowed to pass his examination as Second Mate, after three instead of four years Sea Service.'

The final proof written of the definition 'Quarter Boy', or 'QB', a status or progression no longer available to aspirants to a sea-going career.

Final farewell

Over thirty years later, the boy from Eastbourne returned with his wife to Plas Newydd, with prior knowledge that HMS *Conway* no longer existed, but desirous of discovering whatever roots were still there. The estate was then run by the National Trust, and where once the Captain Superintendent had his quarters, there lived the Marquis and Marchioness, the house being open to the public. That part of the house that was home to *Conway* cadets was run by the Cheshire County Council and gave residence to youth pursuing sailing and mountaineering interests in the area, and was little changed other than the fact that the smell of Ronuk no longer pervaded. The Dock was unchanged except that the slipway had been refurbished, and of course the Pinnace, No. 1 and No. 2 powerboats no longer existed. Gone too were the cutters, but the gigs were still in proud service with HMS *Indefatigable*, the seamen's training school still then operative in the Strait. The Camp was the visitors' car park, but the canteen remained as a proud reminder of the past, still serving meals as a cafeteria to the visiting public. Little had changed inside it, and to eat one's sandwich lunch there was to experience an almost unnerving feeling of time warp, of *déjà vu*, and surely one heard a faint echo in the background that repeated down the years: 'One beans on toast, one cup of coffee, and make it snappy, woman!'

The music room of the Marquis, or Ballroom as it was so incorrectly referred those many years ago, brought back poignant and painful memories of two left-footed attempts at ballroom dancing, as scrubbed and red faced cadets beneath the watchful eye of a Duty Officer stilted their way round the floor, leading, loosely speaking, equally tense young Welsh ladies bussed in from Bangor for those occasions of cultural exposure. Little doubt too that the dancing teacher, doubled in role as chaperon, was aware of the conversation purported to have taken place between a concerned First Lieutenant RN and a self-sure Chief Officer Wren, when discussing such similar social intercourse in Portsmouth.

'Don't worry, my girls have got it up here,' she reassured, tapping her forefinger against her forehead.

'I don't care where they've got it,' he rejoined mournfully, 'my lads are still going to find it!'

In the courtyard of Kelvin Block, or the School Block those years ago, came the exciting discovery that the battle grey classroom huts still stood, although a peek through the windows proved their current role, those years later, as overflow dormitories untidily scattered with evacuated bedding. Sadly, and acting as improvised curtaining, were two HMS *Conway* bunk covers, their *Conway* crest on blue background material still proudly defiant but forlornly misused, and by no means uniformly hung, in their final indignity.

Overall, the heartfelt feeling was that spirit cadets of *Conway* past would be mostly satisfied that their Ship, their home for those years, was in thoughtful and careful hands and whilst the beautifully tended lawns and prolific rhododendron bushes looked somehow lost without squads of perspiring and oilskin clad cadets weaving left–right, left–right between them, it is amazing just what can happen to a place once they stop the Ronuking!

CHAPTER 7

Outward Bound: Ullswater

'TO SERVE, TO STRIVE AND NOT TO YIELD': motto of the Outward Bound Trust.

Provisional acceptance by the P & O demanded successful completion of a one-month course at, in this case, the mountaineering school at Ullswater, run by the Outward Bound Trust, prior to final acceptance.

This appeared at face value somewhat of a doddle after two years at *Conway*, but events proved, that September in 1955, that new challenges were to be imposed to be overcome. Those who came from HMS *Worcester*, Pangbourne, or Warsash likely experienced similar feeling, but now those who had attended different colleges came together for the first time as P & O people, or potentially so, to share a new and common experience.

Rock climbing, fell walking, abseiling, canoeing, athletics, commando course, swimming, and, horribly reminiscent of the morning routine at *Conway*, a 0630 reveille followed by a mind–jerking run to Ullswater lake for a freezing morning plunge. Happily it was September, and the scars on chest of one instructor, seconded from the Marine Commandos as were others, bore mute evidence that someone had to break the ice first during the winter courses! Instant hero-worship.

The almost military regime imposed upon attendees at that time rested easily upon those that had already attended Naval Colleges, but undoubtedly and initially confused many that came from industrial environments. Morning parade, quasi-military drill, the then presence of several Commando instructors and a relatively harsh code of conduct set the scene, but everyone reacted positively, particularly to the assault course, competitively run to challenge each Patrol to complete its length and strength in shorter time than the other. The 'wall' was the worst opposition, and to get a Patrol comprising some twelve people over it in so many seconds came close to breaking bones, spirit and not a few tempers. It seemed to bear little relevance to navigating a large ocean liner around the world, or indeed driving

43

a lathe in Leeds, but it became all consuming in its demand to all, and eventually was satisfactorily mastered.

The first experience of abseiling was startling, and commenced with a sudden leap backward from the high roof of the school building by the Commando Sergeant from Scotland, loosely attached to an adjacent chimney by the flimsiest line that fed over his shoulder, round his buttocks and back through his hands. His swift and safe walk down the red brick vertical wall of the building was viewed with some amazement, but his insistence that the assembled class should now follow his example gave pause for some sincere reappraisal of desire to continue the course.

'I have went down safely,' he intoned with scant regard for grammatical accuracy, and like it or not, all had to take the so-called 'hot seat method' off the roof that forenoon.

He was a magnificent and capable exponent of his craft and an asset to the school, but short on humour. It was therefore a matter of some misfortune that he overheard the tail end of the story whereby a schoolboy, guilty of using the word 'went' when 'gone' should have prevailed, was told to write out one hundred times 'I have gone'. On completion of this exercise, and in temporary absence of the teacher, he left his parting message on the blackboard, thus:

'I have written "I have gone" one hundred times, and have went home.'

'And I've been trained to kill wi' ma bare hands, laddie,' whispered the Sergeant, having crept into the dormitory unobserved, but nevertheless spared the raconteur with singular self control, and went back to his quarters. Over that month, he gained the deepest respect of all, a giant among men.

As time progressed, rock climbing, canoeing and camping out became commonplace, with fell walking over long daily distances now becoming routine. Kendal mint cake and Grapenuts are now probably body intolerable to those on that course, but at the time they served their purpose of sustaining.

Pitching bivouacs in what appeared to be a convenient gully against enticingly handy sheep walls proved a lesson never to be forgotten as torrential rain forced minor flood water over and past the sleeping bags, whilst throwing tealeaves into water yet to boil over the primus proved to be equally disheartening.

Exhilarating canoe expeditions, through white water and swift flowing Cumberland rivers, were only once spoiled by almost too late recognition of barbed wire stretched cynically bank to bank at seated chest level, with consequent frantic back paddling and an actual need to exercise capsize skills so painstakingly imparted by yet another Commando instructor.

There were sudden weather clampdowns, and always the remembered instruction to maintain compass bearings, and in the event, to seek shelter from the wind. That moment of awful truth when faithful to instruction and warning, the patrol halted its crawl through wet clinging fog over the fells when compass bearings became confused:

'I have a sheep's turd under my left hand, is it on the map?'

Moments later, the fog lifted to reveal an almost perpendicular drop of some two hundred feet only inches in front. Perhaps now the realisation was coming that this did indeed have relevance to driving ships and lathes, but regardless, it was a very present challenge.

Athletics and the assault course however held everyone's attention. The former required standards of achievement to be reached successfully to complete the month, and the latter presented constant challenge to each Patrol, for only at the month's end would the fastest Patrol over the course be decided. Evening or spare time became that bloody wall, or the javelin, or the three-mile road run, or the shot putt, but gradually were whittled down by all to just a single athletic event needing that vital 'standard', and the final teams' attempt on the assault course.

For one of the potential P & O cadets, the achievement of standard for the five-mile road run became dangerously elusive, and to the credit of one of the staff, it was insisted that one final attempt be made with him acting as pacemaker on a bicycle. No quarter was given, no slackening of pace allowed and constant jeering reference to inadequacy forced enough animosity into the event to ensure that at the final panting collapse the standard had been achieved. 'Strive, and not to yield.'

The month drew to its hectic close, with final tests of acquired skills in rock climbing, abseiling, canoeing, and long distance fell walking, brought together in the last three-day expedition that ranged the patrols wide over Cumberland, seeking and following carefully prepared and planted clues that would challenge fully each individual in every learned discipline.

Arrival back home weary, footsore and sodden wet to a huge pot of hot stew and mugs of hot sweet tea was blessed relief, in wonderful recognition that no more Grapenuts had to be indulged or mint cake masticated.

From Pooley Bridge through Patterdale, Helvellyn, Borrowdale, Grisedale Pike, Saddleback of Matterdale, and back to Ullswater, teams were guided over, through, up, down, across and throughout by those dedicated instructors from the Outward Bound School, seconded Commandos, thoughtful and deeply responsible members of the various local mountain rescue teams, and mountaineers with no particular interest other than to impart their crafts to those prepared to listen and be guided.

At the final assembly before the Warden, there was a different group from that of a month ago in that backs were straighter, shoulders squarer and overall was a quiet sense of achievement, a pleasant feeling of group accomplishment. Committed to a pledge of no smoking and no alcohol some thirty days before, each course attendee now had to move forward to sign, for the second time, in testimony that that pledge had not been breached. That done, each received, in varying colours according to achievement, a small enameled badge enscribed 'Outward Bound Ullswater', whilst on the reverse was engraved the reminder of course achievement: 'To serve, to strive, and not to yield.'

Each of the P & O potentials (there were four that September at Ullswater) successfully completed the course, and true to promised progression, moved forward to the next square on the board.

CHAPTER 8

Indentures

IN OCTOBER 1955, THE General Office of Register and Records of Shipping and Seamen, in Cardiff, received to its attention 'Indenture for three years Service between a native of Eastbourne (hereafter called the Apprentice) of the first part, and the Peninsular and Oriental Steam Navigation Company of 122 Leadenhall Street, London E.C. (hereinafter called the Company) of the second part.'

It was therein witnessed that the said native of Eastbourne 'hereby voluntarily binds himself Apprentice to the Company for the Term of Three years from the date hereof to serve on any vessel belonging to the Company to which they or their Agents may from time to time appoint him. And the Apprentice hereby covenants that during such time he will faithfully serve the Company, and shall be at all times subject and obedient to the orders of the Company . . . and of the Master or other Officer in command or charge of the vessel . . . and will keep their secrets. And the apprentice will not during the said term do any damage to the Company . . . or to the Master or other Officer of the vessel in which he may be serving, nor will he consent to such damage being done by others, but will if possible prevent the same and give warning thereof; and will not embezzle or waste the goods of the Company . . . nor absent himself without leave, nor frequent taverns or alehouses nor play at unlawful games . . . and do everything in his power to promote the interests of the Company'.

In consideration whereof the Company . . . shall teach him or cause him to be taught the business of a seaman and the duties of a Navigating Officer in the Company's vessels and provide the Apprentice with sufficient board, but not wines or spirits, beer or liquors. And the Apprentice shall live in such place in the vessel as may be assigned to him. The Company will provide sufficient bedding and table linen for the Apprentice, but he shall provide himself with sufficient and suitable wearing apparel and other necessaries. A premium of Fifty Pounds shall be paid to the Company on the date of signing Indenture. A portion of this sum shall be returned to the Surety if the conduct of the Apprentice is satisfactory. In addition, the following payments shall be made to the Apprentice, viz One Hundred and Thirty Pounds, One Hundred and Fifty Pounds, One Hundred and Seventy Five Pounds at the end of the first, second and third years respectively.

To the Indenture was appended the information that the Apprentice was 'Ex HMS *Conway*, Full Course Completed', but sadly no similar reference to having scaled the odd mountain or two, meantime.

An Acting Secretary named MacKenzie made his mark for the P & O, and the young native of Eastbourne on his own young behalf.

On 10 October 1955, a determination to enter the service of the 'Coldstream Guards of the Merchant Service' became reality. The deed was done.

From 'Quit ye like men, be strong', through 'To serve, to strive, and not to yield', to that most portentous of mottos that now inspired and led: 'QUIS NOS SEPARABIT'! Who, indeed.

1. *Summer Term 1955. L–R Sir Donald Anderson, Deputy Chairman Peninsular & Oriental Steam Navigation Company; Deputy Chief Cadet Captain Perry; Chief Cadet Captain Swanson; Captain E. Hewitt RD, RNR, Captain Superintendent*

2. *HMS Conway – hard aground by Menai Bridge*

3. Sad ending to a proud ship

4. Chief Cadet Captain Swanson flanked by Senior Cadet Captain Bartram (left)
and Senior Cadet Captain Dale. Summer Term 1955

5. *Cadet Holmes with ship's figurehead supine ashore*

6. *Re-masted ashore*

7. *Plas Newydd, with view of the Boathouse Tryst*

8. *HMS* Conway *3rd XV, Christmas Term 1954. Back row: Mr K. Bayliss, J.M. May, R.W. Douglas, D. Batten, T.I.H. Phipps, B.E. Pritchard, A.R. Gill, B.S. Dale. Middle row: T. Soovere, D.O. Christie, I.C. Munro (Capt.), H. Dutton, E.G. Puddifer. Front row: G.M. Laverick, J.W. Perry, B.G. Mavity, A.J.M. Swanson. Played 8. Won 7. Lost 1. Points for 133. Points against 27*

9. Sunday Divisions

10. The camp, post grounding of the ship

11. *Upper Fifth Class, Spring Term 1955. Back row: Pickup, Rahman, Wallin, Turner. 3rd row: Watson, Grant, Holmes, Orme, Owen, Bartram. 2nd row: Perry, Slee, McGarr, Swanson, Woods, Islam, Wilson. Front row: Douglas, Martin, Sinkinson*

12. Quarter Boys, Summer Term 1955

SENIOR CADET CAPTAINS

Chief Cadet Captain	A. J. M. Swanson.		Mizzentop	S. Redmond.
Deputy Chief Cadet Captain	J. W. Perry.		Hold	P. Pickup.
Forecastle	J. A. Turner.		Games	F. Martin.
Foretop	B. S. Dale.		Sailing	C. C. Hufflett.
Maintop	A.C.G. Bartram.		Mess Deck	R.N.E. Oakes.

• • •

CADETS LEFT JULY, 1955

Name	Company	Name	Company
Atkinson, K.I.	Manchester Liners.	Oakes, R.N.E.	Natal Line.
Bartram, A.C.G.	Blue Star Line.	Orme, D.F.	Alfred Holt & Co.
Chappell, J.L.	Civil Life.	Owens, J.H.	Andrew Weir.
Cole, W.	Port Line.	Perry, J.W.	P. & O. Line.
Cubbin, R.J.	Union Castle Line.	Pickup, P.	Alfred Holt & Co. (Engineer Cadet).
Douglas, R.W.	Royal Mail Lines Ltd.	Rahman, Q.A.B.M.M.	Mackinnon MacKenzie.
Dutton, H.	Houlder Brothers.	Redman, D.A.	South American Saint Line.
Feasey, D.P.	Houlder Brothers.	Redmond, S.	Royal Fleet Auxiliary.
Gibbins, A.N.	Elder Dempster (Purser Cadet).	Roberts, D.A.	Orient Line (Purser Cadet).
Grant, B.	Blue Star Line.	Sharp, J.W.	Bibby Line.
Hayes, B.	Civil Life, Natal.	Sinclair, A.G.	Royal Canadian Navy.
Holmes, G.E.N.	Shaw Savill & Albion.	Sinkinson, G.	Furness Withy.
Hooley, D.S.	Civil Life.	Slee, C.H.V.	Canadian Pacific Steamship Co.
Houghton, D.J.	British Tanker Co.	Speed, A.J.	Clan Line.
Hufflett, C.C.	New Zealand Shipping Co.	Swanson, A.J.M.	Civil Life, Australia.
Hughes, T.	Royal Fleet Auxiliary.	Turner, J.A.	South American Saint Line.
Islam S.M.A.	Mackinnon MacKenzie.	Wallin, G.P.	Clan Line.
Langridge, W.N.	British Tanker Company.	Watson, I.G.	Port Line.
McGarr, N.K.	British Tanker Co. (Engineer Cadet).	Whitehouse, J.P.	Cunard Line (Purser Cadet).
McWalter, D.N.	Shell Tankers.	Wilkins, J.M.M.	Royal Fleet Auxiliary.
Martin, F.	T. & J. Harrison.	Wilson, D.F.	Alfred Holt & Co.
Morris, C.E.	Purser Cadet.	Woods, D.W.	Blue Star Line.
Munro, I.C.	Union Castle Line.		

CHAPTER 9

Transition

LIKE MOST OF ITS FIFTIES SUBSTANCE, the then Head Office of the P & O has disappeared under demolition hammers. It then, however, resided in its famed '122' section of Leadenhall Street, London, entered past imposing wrought iron gates, over a surprisingly small forecourt featuring an iron turntable set into its surface (presumably to turn the Chairman's carriage within the narrow confines) and up a short flight of sweeping steps to large Victorian doors.

Within these hallowed walls resided, among untold others, the Sea Staff Personnel Manager, white-haired, and father figure to cadets whom he was to appoint to vessels, guide, remonstrate with, and generally shepherd over their three years of apprenticeship. His name was George, which seemed eminently suitable to his personality, although naturally forbidden in direct usage from his young flock. It was his careful direction that pointed new intakes from more northern colleges toward tailors regularly accustomed to clothing officers of the P & O in prescribed company uniform, and in the case of the *Conway* entrant, to S.W. Silver and Company of Eastcheap. The Sailors' Home of Liverpool had been an amusing distraction, but patently *de trop* under the circumstances.

Here too was the beginning of a twelve year association with a tailor's representative known universally throughout the P & O Company merely, but respectfully, as Mr Errington, and it was from him that the seemingly endless purchase of uniform articles over the coming years now commenced.

Two years at *Conway* had been served well by initial purchases, but

'Really, sir, the No. I uniform suit must of course be replaced now (although you should retain the old one for day-to-day usage once we have changed to P & O buttons), and we must consider the immediate requirement of tropical shorts, shirts, socks, shoes and so forth. It would be opportune to open a banking account, sir, for although we are well accustomed to granting credit to the young

49

gentlemen, we would recommend it as prudent to allow a facility for regular servicing of your account.'

The P & O cap badge, then gold anchor half prone and surmounted by gold rising sun, was reverently added to the growing pile that represented first attainment of 'a tailor's bill', but was viewed perhaps with some concern by one now accustomed to the Royal Navy cap badge of Her Majesty. Momentary flash of mental comparison between the two badges was resolutely put aside as unworthy and immature, and attention paid to the next item, disappointingly devoid of the glamour usually inherent in 'The Company'. A white boiler suit.

'Really?'

'Yes, sir, really,' he solemnly intoned, 'and are you suitably furnished otherwise with sufficient working apparel?' Here the Sailors' Home was thankfully, if only temporarily, adequate.

The unexpected last addition to P & O 'required purchases' was a small book, priced at 4 shillings or thereabouts, written by one C.T. Wilson of the Bombay Pilot Service in 1920 and entitled *The Malim Sahib's Hindustani*, produced 'for ship's officers who wish to acquire a working knowledge of low Hindustani spoken by native crews, coolies, servants and longshoremen generally. All nautical terms and words in common use both ashore and afloat are included.' Or perhaps more provocatively in prefaced explanation, 'in conversation with Lascars and all other low-caste Natives of India who speak the Bazaar "bat".'

Wide-eyed, and temporarily distracted from his original shopping purpose, the Cadet or 'Chota Sahib' as he now realised himself to be, read on.

'One does not need to draw very fine distinctions when speaking to Lascars or Coolies. Indeed, the use of correct grammar to them would in many cases only serve to render the speaker quite unintelligible. It is the opinion of the author that much of the seeming stupidity of the natives is due to the atrocious blunders so constantly occurring in the phrases bellowed at them by the irate Sahib.'

That P & O vessels (save for the *Aden*) were manned by Indian crews had been realised, but this curried breath of colonial advice was the first indication of any language barrier, or indeed need to learn an Eastern language, and excitement mounted.

Escape was finally made from the hushed and dangerously expensive premises of Those Bespoke to Tailor into the bustle of the City, there to seek out means of opening a bank account. Interviews were now commonplace, and it therefore came as no great surprise to learn that the manager of the Midland Bank (Aldgate), his house chosen for its Fenchurch Street proximity to Leadenhall Street and Eastcheap, required to interview the young man intent upon bestowing his custom.

Completely unmoved by the revelation that this potential account was now of the P & O, he chose to warn of the perils that his bank could unleash upon those who, perhaps inadvertently, deviated from the path of economic awareness. He then bade his new account reluctant, and suspicious, welcome.

That was the Talking Bank; the Listening Bank was yet to be launched.

Some weeks later, Mr Errington's smooth diplomacy was overheard to avoid, at least temporarily, a young Engineer Officer clashing with his chosen bank, having purchased his prerequisites of uniform. The latter's apprenticeship with British Rail had apparently not schooled him in the basics of receipts or disbursements.

'That, sir, would appear to represent a purchase of £200, and would you wish to indicate means of payment?'

'I'll write you a cheque.'

'Ah, yes, but I do believe you indicated some moments ago that you have opened a bank account with £50 deposit?'

'Yes, but they have given me a cheque book and so I can pay you with a cheque.'

'With respect, sir, the banking system is somewhat more constrained in its attitude towards usage of cheque facilities than perhaps we would generally applaud, so perhaps a cash deposit of some 5 per cent with appropriate monthly instruction would better suffice your purpose?'

Whether or not that approach contributed to the final demise of S.W. Silver and Company is not known, but it certainly gained many a 'tailor's bill'!

It is perhaps appropriate at this state to develop the matter of P & O Officers' uniforms, as they were then quite distinctively different from those of other Merchant Navy Shipping Lines who sported generally the gold arm-braid of the standard Merchant Navy uniform. Not so the P & O or, indeed, the Orient Line that was to become part of the P & O in a few short years.

Arm-braid for Deck Officers was non-existent, distinctive braid denoting rank being in fact worn on the shoulders. Not, however, as one might assume, in the standard epaulette style as with the Royal Navy in tropical uniform.

The Ship's Commanding Officer (Captain, Commander or Master as you will) wore on each shoulder a gold band, approximately one inch wide and some four inches in length, that ran parallel with, and adjacent to, the seam connecting the upper sleeve to the shoulder pad. To this band attached a gold rising sun emblem. The Fleet Commodore would wear his gold band at double the named width to indicate his elevated status, whilst a Staff Captain (ostensibly second in command of a passenger ship) would wear the Captain's band but minus the rising sun emblem.

The Chief Officer, in common with Merchant Navy practice, displayed three gold stripes, but here the difference continued. In place of the Captain's gold band would be (of similar length and width) a blue band, the three gold stripes running at right angles to the shoulder seam (to the run of the shoulder) achieving therefore only one approximate inch of gold to each stripe. The Second Officer would have two such stripes, the Third Officer one, and the Fourth Officer a single stripe of only half the normal width. Radio Officers, in similarity to the Royal Navy, had green distinctive cloth separating the gold, Pursers white, and Doctors red. Strangely, Engineer Officers wore their distinctive braid on the arm.

(It was said that this style of distinguishing rank stemmed from the need of the ship's lookout at the masthead to identify rank of the officer on deck in days of sail, but not too much credence can be allowed to that theory.)

The cap badge too was completely different from standard Merchant Navy, comprising a gold anchor half prone surmounted by a gold rising sun. Gold uniform buttons were designed in the fashion of the Royal Navy, but instead of a crown surmounting the anchor, again the P & O's ubiquitous rising sun.

For the Cadet, little of this distinctiveness, save of course for the cap badge and buttons. The flashes of white at lapel buttonholes were sadly much smaller than the bold patches of the Royal Naval Midshipman (or even Blue Funnel Midshipman for that matter).

Tailors and banks had their obvious place in the scheme of things, but more importantly, at least to officialdom, was the need to obtain from a Mercantile Marine Office a 'Seaman's Record Book and Certificate of Discharge'.

From the City, descent had to be made to a first exposure to Victoria Docks, and to experience the extraordinary importance that staff of such offices bestowed upon themselves in casual pursuit of their calling. An eye-sight colour test was deemed mandatory (the lantern test), despite documented medical evidence to full visual competence, and was held in a darkened room using hopelessly outdated equipment.

'Call the colour of lights that will show on the screen,' intoned the clerk, and worked his machine.

'Red.'

'Correct.'

'Green.'

'Correct.'

'Yellow.'

'That's not yellow, it's white.' A trace of petulance.

'From where I view, it's yellow. Sorry.'

'That's because the light is distorted by the oil. It's white.' Authority speaks.

Agreement was reached as to the light's whiteness, and the test passed.

Next came the need to photograph the intended holder of the Record Book, and a wooden board with official letter and numbers was held, convict-like, under the model's chin. R643947. Necessary days later, a Discharge Book with convict 'photograph of holder' was disdainfully handed to the new P & O Apprentice, stamped R643974.

'Why is the number on the photograph different from the Book?' Polite enquiry.

'Bloody hell, give it back 'ere', and with tongue protruding carefully between teeth, officialdom from Victoria Docks scratched through the photographed R643947 with careful red ink pen, and wrote *twice* across the photograph the correct number R643974. Two writes make a wrong right, right?

It is probably fair to remark that suspicion seemed to exist in the minds of Board of Trade officialdom relative to P & O Cadets in those days, although undoubtedly P & O treated, and trained, their young intake seriously with the very real intent to have them competently officer their vessels once Indentured time was over.

This was also true of some Board of Trade Examiners who seemed somehow convinced that a P & O Cadet had little or no practical experience of basic seamanship, having spent his entire three years Indenture swanning it up on passenger vessels. Alternatively, it was presumed that he had spent an inordinate amount of his three years on bridge watch duties, unleavened by chipping hammer, three cornered scraper and wire brush, together with cocktails of red lead, tallow and wire dressing grease. The fact that P & O had Indian crews heightened the image, the Board of Trade seemingly concerned that a P & O Cadet served as only another link in the chain of command in achieving ship husbandry work, with no direct hands-on involvement.

Let it be said that few P & O Cadets sought to disillusion them from these preconceived ideas (except of course in final oral examinations before the dreaded Examiner of Masters and Mates, where no hiding place existed in fable), so one probably took more ribaldry or antagonism than most as he moved through the three years of Apprenticeship, at least from outside the cloistered ranks of P & O. Stories abounded of would-be P & O 2nd Mates astonishing Examiners with their drawled and addle-pated response to questions of seamanship.

'Describe a derrick heel block to me, boy.'

'A heel block, sir?'

'Yes, a heel block.'

'Well, sir, it's, ur, red.' (A reference to the fact that indeed in P & O cargo ships, blocks were painted a rust-like colour.)

Or:

'Describe what steps you would take to erect sheerlegs.' Always a testing question.

'Well, sir, I would simply instruct the Serang to rig sheerlegs, sir.'

'No, as Cadets we are not allowed to wear the P & O Officer's sword,' another mythical reference.

None of it was true of course, but always defended, tongue in cheek, as highly likely.

The majority of the three year apprenticeship would be spent in the P & O cargo ship fleet that sailed in three main tradelanes, namely India, Australasia and the Far East and of the three (ironically perhaps in view of P & O's association with the Sub-Continent) India was viewed by most as the worst to achieve in appointment, being serviced by the slowest and smallest ships in the fleet. These ships were seemingly destined to spend sometimes intolerable lengths of time in Colombo (that wasn't too bad, with much cricket and so forth to be played), Calcutta, Vizagaputnan, Madras and oft-times en route in such as Port Sudan. The ships deployed in 1955 were the *Cannanore*, *Coramandel*, *Kyber*, *Karmala*, *Socotra*, *Devanha* and *Dongola*, the last two famous for their ability to make sternway in a head wind!

Of greater attraction were those ships, much fleeter of foot and larger to boot, that sailed to Australasia, to the land of fabled milk and honey.

If the new young intake Cadets were to believe it, beaches and parties awaited, with nubile young Australian girls to sweet talk them (well, that's perhaps going too far), though barbecues, tennis, horse riding and golf, and months on the Australian coast were to be gently whiled away as the Australian 'wharfies' exerted their right to strike on a shift by shift basis. Not for these ships the squalid waters of the Hoogli river, or the continued slap of gobuled beetlenut juice onto their wooden decks, but rather the clean deep waters of the Pacific which crashed thunderously, thence sparkling and chuckling onto glistening white beaches, whilst the harbours of Australia and New Zealand reportedly stopped only yards short from a beckoning friendliness that awaited just down the gangway.

Together with the poor old *Aden*, this tradelane was served by the *Ballarat* and *Bendigo*, *Perim*, *Patonga* and *Pinjarra*, who as an added attraction would oft-times share brief port time with their big sister passenger liners in Sydney, Melbourne, Adelaide and Fremantle. To the delight of the officers manning the cargo ships, they were usually invited to sample the liners' laden lunch and dinner tables, not to forget the few gins beforehand.

Tales of the Far East were also singularly more attractive than those of the Indian Sub-Continent, with the fabled Malaya (to include Singapore) and Hong Kong to look forward to, with tantalising hints of geishas and Turkish baths closely entwined with the name of Japan, evocative and mysterious in itself. Fujiama, Hiroshima, Yokohama, Tokyo, Kobe, and the Japanese Inland Sea. There would be cherry blossom, cultured pearls and sampans, together with cameras and electrical equipment at ridiculously low prices. All this and more to the lucky ones appointed to this run, served by vessels such as the *Shillong, Singapore, Surat, Somali, Sunda* and *Soudan*, all, and not unlike their Australian sisters, of superior speed and size to those employed toward India.

It was, however, no matter of choice as to where an appointment was made, at least not to the Cadets. It was a matching of who was available for appointment to those berths that had become open owing to a variety of reasons, present incumbents fortunate enough to be selected for transfer to a cruise liner during the Mediterranean cruising season, completion of indentures, or just plain 'due leave'.

Those who had now become indentured therefore awaited news of their first appointment, with undisguised impatience, not a little apprehension, and an almost total lack of awareness of what was really to be expected of them. Pre-sea training and Outward Bounding had prepared them for a naval college environment and the ability to scale mountains and the disciplines that all that entailed. The rest was to come. They were about to go down to the sea in P & O ships.

Nor indeed had anything prepared any of them for the Tilbury and Royal group of docks in London's East End, home port of the P & O fleet save for the summer cruising season, when the great white liners, deployed to the Mediterranean, would temporarily shift to the more wholesome port of Southampton.

Approach to the Royal Albert, King George V or Victoria Docks, along mean and dirty roads livened only by the bright flash of the red London Transport 101 bus, was immensely depressing and a far fling from the bracing air of North Wales or the heady atmosphere of Cumberland. Grime was all pervading, and an air of sullenness apparent, almost tangible enough to touch.

The portly Port of London Authority police (they all seemed portly) who guarded the Dock gates reflected an attitude that anyone going into the Docks was a prime candidate to attempt smuggling something out (probably true of the majority of London's dockers who then saw pilferage of cargo as part of their remuneration package), and treated accordingly. The sullen oily swirl of foul smelling water within the Docks themselves, hardly relieved by the tidal ordained opening of the Docks' bowels (the locks), completed the ugly initial impression, the movement of ships somehow synonymous in their passing into the River Thames of gut relief, of escape to eventually cleaner waters.

Bustle and movement there was, however, as cranes swayed and swung to the rhythm of commerce, loading and discharging the many cargo holds that lay open before them, the ships nose to tail in dirty resignation to the intrusion of their innards. Tugs nudged and snatched at myriad barges as they jostled for position to or from the sea-going vessels, or responded to the whistled and hooted instructions of the Dock pilots, and churned the evil smelling waters of the Docks into turgid movement as ships entered or left the Port. Trucks in continuous noisy stream, the landside equivalent of the barges in purpose, hauled their loads to and from the tender care and handling of London's dockers, that cloth-capped and heavy booted fraternity who wielded their cargo hooks, often with practised intent to defraud.

There was a continuous harsh cacophony of sound and swirl of movement, deadened or silenced only by the gaseous mantle of thick yellowy fog that would oft-times blanket and hide, or the light spatter of rain that with its awesome wetness could persuade lusty dockers into instant immobility, and the docks into massive camp-like areas as hatch tents were hastily erected. Merchant Navy Officers would solemnly notate their working log, 'Rain commenced 1500 hours, hatch tents rigged.' The P & O Officer wrote, 'Rain stopped play, wickets covered.'

Notwithstanding the trade-route, India, Australasia or the Far East, this was nevertheless the start point, and to this grimy bustle of a place came the new P & O Cadets all gleamy clean and keen, each to his appointed vessel, arrival at the bottom of the ship's gangway somehow symbolic of the fact that no matter what heights of achievement had been reached at training college, he now stood at the bottom of another ladder. First trip Cadet, a 'New Chum' all over again.

The suggestion that this place would become some thirty plus years later an airport where stood now cargo sheds, or the evil waters a centre for water sports, would have had the perpetrator swiftly bundled away by white coated attendants. It was beyond belief.

Extract from P & O Regulations, reprint dated 31 October 1956. 'General Outline of the Duties of Certain Individual Officers' Section 10: CADETS.

Whether P & O Cadets are trained with care and imagination, or casually, is of vital importance to the Company. These young men are our Deck Officers of the future. They must be guided and taught not only their professional duties, but equally important, the outlook and habits of an Officer and, there is no better word, gentleman. Habits learned now may persist, for good or for ill, for life, and what habits are learned will depend much on the example set by their seniors. Not everyone has a flair for guiding youth, but let all realise at least how important this guidance is. The Commander above all should get to know the Cadets, and should ensure for them a blend of sensible discipline, progressive professional work, and a leavening of relaxation and social life ashore, where it can be arranged.

Cadets are to be instructed and trained in accordance with Appendix B and as far as possible in conformity with the procedure laid down by the Merchant Navy Training Board.

Extract from P & O Regulations, reprint dated 31 October 1956. Appendix 'B.' CADETS

These instructions are issued for the guidance of Commanders, and they are to be carried out as circumstances permit.

Watches and Duties at Sea.
Cadets are to be divided into three watches at sea, and employed on the following duties with a view to profitable training and acquiring the necessary knowledge of their profession.

Practical Navigation.
Cadets are to be given opportunity and assistance to practise chart work and the taking of sights and azimuths. They should be instructed in the use and upkeep of all navigational instruments and other aids to navigation.

Work Book.

An ordinary navigational work book is to be used for all practical navigation, examination exercises, correspondence course exercises and essays. This book should be inspected and initialled weekly by the Commander or Supervising Officer.

Journal.

A concise and neatly written journal is to be kept by all Cadets. This book is to contain only such work as may be useful to the Cadet for his examination for his Second Mate's certificate and for his subsequent career as an Officer. It should contain the following subjects:

Details of the ship in which he is working – with sketches.

Cargo methods of working at ports visited – port and ship organisation – stowage plans and cargo records – details of heavy lifts and heavy lifting gear.

Mail and baggage – organisation and stowage.

Anchors and cables – methods of mooring and anchoring at ports visited, with illustrations.

Methods of berthing at ports visited.

Navigation notes, and drawings of landfalls, harbours etc. Use of navigational instruments, sextant, chronometers, magnetic and gyro compasses, sounding machines, patent logs, radio D/F, radar.

Use and upkeep of life saving equipment and fire fighting appliances.

Management of boats under oars and sails – power boats.

Care and maintenance of the ship.

Examples of seamanship.

Exercises in Hindustani.

This book is to be forwarded to the Nautical Inspector at the termination of each voyage and should be signed by the Commander and Supervising Officer. After inspection by the Nautical Inspector, it will be returned to the owner.

Correspondence Course.

All Cadets, on entry, will be enrolled for a correspondence course of instruction prepared by the King Edward VII Nautical College, London. The following arrangements have been made:

1. All correspondence between the school and the Cadet is to pass through the Nautical Inspector.

2. The Nautical Inspector to be responsible for the distribution of the lesson books.
3. On completion of each lesson book, the text papers are to be sent by Company's despatch box or airmail direct to the Nautical Inspector, who will forward this to the school for marking.
4. The Cadet will commence each voyage with books to cover six months' work.

In order to facilitate the smooth working of the scheme, the Officer appointed to supervise the studies of the Cadets is to make himself conversant with the instructions issued with the course. The course will relieve the Instructing Officer of most of the theoretical side of the training, but he will be responsible for the general supervision of the studies required by the course, also for the practical training and for the instruction in subjects not covered by the course.

First Aid, Principles of Hygiene and Matters of Physical Interest.
The Surgeon should be encouraged to give lectures in these subjects as opportunities occur.

In Port.
Entering or leaving port, Cadets are to be stationed on the Bridge, Forecastle and Poop, in order to gain knowledge of manoeuvring, mooring and unmooring ship. When working cargo, they are to be employed in the holds, or as required.

Leave in Port.
Is granted by the Commander, to whom applications are to be made.

Report of Qualifications and Progress.
At the termination of each voyage, a report on the conduct of the Cadets, qualification etc. is to be entered on the Officers' Report Form by the Commander. In addition, he is to furnish a special letter giving fuller particulars regarding the following:
   Application to study, attention to duties, promise as a navigator, and above all, the character of the Cadet. It is character, more than anything else, that will determine whether or not he will ultimately be fit for command in the Company's service. Comment should be made on any subjects in connection with which the Cadet has shown particular aptitude.

Quarters.
Cadets are to keep their quarters clean and tidy, and these will be inspected regularly.

CHAPTER 10

The Indian Run: *Cannanore*

THE *CANNANORE*, HUDDLED ALONGSIDE No. 11 berth King George V Dock looked huge: huge, black-hulled and indescribably dirty, with the slap marks of dusty rope slings marking her sides, and the rust of previous voyages bleeding from her hull and upper works. Hatch boards littered her main deck, and London's all-pervading grime had been trampled into her wooden boat deck by the uncaring boots of many dockers. Black speckles of dirt, droppings of industrial fog and rain, mottled the buff paint of the accommodation and bridge superstructure, and she was overall a lump in the throat disappointment to the young Cadet who gazed up the grubby Port of London Authority wooden gangway that gave access to the main deck above him.

In fact she was not large, merely larger than life previously experienced, and indeed at some 7,000 gross tons weight and 485 feet length, quite small. She and her sister ship *Coromandel* had both been built in 1949 by Barclay Curle of Glasgow and despite present appearances, were not old, their respective Doxford diesel engines having pushed them to and from India for a mere five years of service. A far cry from the great white liners, she was nevertheless a P & O vessel, and a brief climb up the PLA gangway found the first evidence of this, in the shape of a smiling dark-skinned Secunny, or Indian Quartermaster, dressed in quasi-naval uniform, his jet-black hair surmounted by what appeared to be a home-made naval rating's hat with the proud letters *CANNANORE*, in gold, on its black ribboned circumference.

'Salaam, sahib,' he greeted, his manner of address hiding his knowledge of the uncertainty that was displayed before him.

'Eh, good morning, can you show me to the Chief Officer's office?' responded the Cadet, his brief glance at Malim Sahib's Hindustani beforehand being completely negated by this sudden confrontation with 'BAT'. Written instructions from Leadenhall Street had been specific: that upon joining he should report to the

61

Chief Officer, and that at least was something tangible to grasp at amid the awful confusion caused by the culture shock of East Ham and Royal Docks, the latter so inappropriately named if appearances were to be judged.

The Secunny nodded, and with a glance down the gangway to reassure himself that the Cadet's trunk was in no immediate danger of being stolen, led the way from the gangway forward to the accommodation entrance, a heavily built wooden door giving access to the dark wood panelled interior.

This, the *Cannanore*, or *'Cunning Whore'* as she was more affectionately referred to, was to be the Cadet's home for the next ten months and twenty days, save for brief home leave between voyages, and experience gained later in joining other vessels was to confirm that she was a happy ship. Whilst not realising it at the time, there is an inherent atmosphere to every ship that speaks of good or bad will, harsh or fair discipline, camaraderie or tension, and *Cannanore* whispered well through her being while the muted rumble of her auxiliary engines spoke well of her lot, despite her present incarceration in London Docks.

Audience with the Chief Officer, a quiet spoken Australian of medium build and lived-in face, was brief, pressed as he was by Shore Superintendents and his own coastal relief officer, all intent on handing over the vessel prior to her departure for the deep-sea voyage, and making a visible effort to realise the end of his meagre dock supply of gin. The Senior Cadet was therefore called for, with instruction to organise the new lad aboard, and to introduce him to the workings of the vessel, his fellow Cadets and his immediate duties, bearing in mind that he was to be allocated to the 8–12 watch. Thus, and almost as an anti-climax to the build-up over the last few hectic weeks, were the new intake of Cadets quietly absorbed into their appointed vessels.

The hustle and bustle of final cargo loading, last minute storing and 'signing on', together with the arrival back from leave of the resident Captain and officers, appeared to give doubt to the fact that such a voyage had ever been undertaken before, or indeed was likely to actually happen at all. A bowler-hatted gentleman in shiny blue suit and raincoat appeared to own the vessel, if his demands for attention were anything to go by, and only the timely information that this was the Shore Superintendent saved a Cadet the embarrassment of telling the noisome creature to push off. Apparently he did own the vessel. It was probably Mr Errington of S.W. Silver & Co. who imparted the information, as he quietly went about his business of supplying the forgotten pairs of white canvas uniform shoes or the black cummerbund for 'Red Sea rig', omitted somehow in the original purchase of 'absolutely necessary' items of uniform. Or it may have been the representative from the Merchant Navy and Airline Officers' Association but that is less likely as he was equally noisome, but in a less professional way, and was indeed quite often told to push off!

The duties of a P & O Cadet were many and varied as it quickly became apparent, and all were designed to progress him towards the eventual and successful passing of his first professional examination (2nd Mate's Certificate) and to attain appointment as a Junior Officer. The Cadets' responsibility for looking after the four racehorses that were landed in their horseboxes onto the deck next to No. 4 hatch did however come as somewhat of a surprise to the newcomer, such activity not having been covered at pre-sea Training College; that the horses also seemed apprehensive was obvious as they had undoubtedly not been informed of their transfer from Newmarket to Colombo, or indeed that their new lads were more accustomed to mucking out with a Ronuk machine than a pitchfork. The final arrival of a Great Dane, to be kenneled on the appropriately named poop deck, completed the definition of that voyage's veterinary duties, which fortunately fell to the lot of a Cadet from the School of Navigation Warsash, who by sheer coincidence was, in later years, to take up pig-farming!

As in most P & O cargo ships, the four Cadets were quartered (no pun really intended) in a four-berth cabin with a small study adjacent. The latter was intended, as the name implies, as a place for the study of the correspondence courses that had to be completed by various stages during the voyage, under the tutorial eye of the Third Officer. In fact, and in view of limited space in the cabin (two double bunks scarcely separated by a chest of drawers) the study became an off-duty living room, where people had very quickly to learn to live with each other in an environment that wasn't about to go away.

Inter-college rivalry that might have existed generally devolved into an interest in how the other college had worked, or in the case of the *Conway* Cadet, an opportunity to find out if the Duty Watch at Pangbourne really had mowed the lawns. One Cadet's interest in classical music in *Cannanore* drove most to initial distraction, but led to eventual enjoyment. The Pangbourne Cadet's insistence on having a caged budgie was rationalised into daily secret speech lessons to the extent that Billy the Budgie very soon became the self-proclaimed Billy the Bastard until, one day, no doubt infuriated by his own foul language and an overpowering desire for more space, he flew out of the cabin window (yes window, not porthole) proclaiming his birthright to a vast and totally indifferent North Sea, never to be seen again.

Such close proximity gave little hiding place for personal secrets or emotions, and nicknames achieved during college days, so gratefully discarded on graduation, somehow seemed to come back to haunt. One ex-*Worcester* boy, not best liked owing to his unfortunate inability to handle his Senior Cadet status, coupled with a nasal bray of a laugh, was defensive in this regard, during one voyage.

'You'd only laugh if I told you, so what's the point?'

With the tongue in cheek total assurance to the contrary, delivered by his spellbound audience of three, and no doubt loosened by one of his allowed two beers a day, he finally conceded.

'Panties,' he confided.

'What?' from three disbelieving mouths.

'Panties,' he confirmed, and stormed in pique from the cabin as his three shipmates fell about roaring with laughter, tears streaming down their cheeks. The name was to dog him for years to come.

The Duties of the Cadet, or Apprentice if you will, were essentially governed by the learning curve as previously referred to, and in that regard the P & O Company went about its business of creating their new officers in a dedicated and professional manner, allowing them a dignity meanwhile that was seldom seen in other merchant fleets. The easiest course was to have Cadets, cheap labour as could be considered, doing or achieving nothing but deckhands' work with but the occasional view of the navigating bridge perhaps on a Sunday at sea, and this course was indeed followed by too many Companies to their great detriment, and indeed disgrace.

P & O had some fifty to sixty Navigating Cadets on their strength during the fifties and each had to pursue continued academic studies through the Company sponsored correspondence course during the three year sea-going Indenture, and to ensure that noses were kept to the grindstone, each vessel with a complement of Cadets had one officer (usually the 3rd Officer) accountable for progress and submissions on a timely basis. Moreover, Chief Officers were charged with the responsibility to ensure that bridge watch-keeping time was in sensible proportion to day-work, which latter entailed anything from scaling, painting, scrubbing, varnishing, splicing and canvas sewing to lifeboat maintenance, bilge cleaning, derrick maintenance and wire dressing. Or, and in the particular case of *Cannanore*, manning the 'chains' when entering some Indian ports to magnificently heave the lead to check channel depth.

Thus for all coastal voyages in home waters, and all periods of close coasting *en voyage*, Cadets would be allocated to bridge watch-keeping routine to assist, and indeed learn from, the officer in charge of the particular watch. Similarly in port, watches would be maintained but for the purpose of properly supervising the safe and prudent load/discharge of cargo, and for the Cadet to gain first-hand practical knowledge of that important aspect of his Company's interests. On deep-sea passages too, it was normal for at least one Cadet (usually the most senior) to stand full watches to gain practical experience in sun and star navigation.

P & O, in common with most Merchant Companies, worked the three watch system (8–12, 12–4, 4–8), not working the 'dog watch' system adopted by the Royal Navy that ensured watch keeping officers rang the changes. Which officer stood which watch was really at the Captain's dictate and largely depended in the cargo ships as to whether he was comfortable with the Fourth Officer standing his own watch (as the most junior officer), or whether he would insist that the Chief Officer took a watch with the most junior as his 'winger'.

In the *Cannanore*, the Captain chose the latter option, which thus gave the Third Officer the 8–12 watch, the Second Officer the 12–4 (or death watch) and the Chief Officer/Fourth Officer, the 4–8. This suggested no incompetence on the part of the Fourth Officer, but was rather reflective of the Captain's need to gauge his new officer's capabilities, particularly as the officer concerned was one of those rare cases in the then P & O who had joined the Company not as a Cadet, but already qualified.

The Royal Navy 'slips and proceeds to sea', but that is somehow
not at all synonymous with merchant ships' sequence of sailing
events, although the P & O probably came the closest to it, at least
in terms of ceremony. Despite *Cannanore*'s ghastly departure hours of
2 a.m. from the Royal Docks, the only uniform concession was that
officers were permitted to wear white rollneck sweaters rather than
the customary collar and tie, and an officer's blue beret (with badge
affixed) was acceptable instead of a uniform cap.

With 'Hands to stations for leaving harbour' called, the Third
Officer proceeded to the forecastle with his Cadet and Indian crew
members, the Second Officer aft, and the Chief Officer, Fourth
Officer and remaining watch-keeping Cadet to the bridge, there to
dance attendance upon the Captain and Pilot as the ship was let go,
and pulled from the dockside by Sun tugs that belched their odious
funnel contents squarely over these attending ropes and lines. Whilst
tugs stirred vile smells from the dock waters with their churning
propellers, *Cannanore*'s own propeller thrashed as her Engineer
Officers responded to bridge telegraph, and turning short round in
her own length, she proceeded slowly towards the waiting locks that
were finally to disgorge her to the sullen Thames, and eventually the
freedom of the sea.

This was a deep-sea voyage, and course was set through the Dover
Strait and English Channel to Ushant, and so to the Bay of Biscay;
south-west to Cape Finisterre and thence south to Cape St Vincent,
turning easterly to pass through the Strait of Gibraltar and into the
Mediterranean, a voyage to that point of some 1,200 nautical miles
or close to four days at *Cannanore*'s rather sedate 13 knots of speed.

This was to become familiar territory over the coming years, but
to the new Cadets it was fascinating in every aspect, each day
bringing new experiences with always the prospect of more on the
morrow. *Cannanore*, in common with others, sloughed off the grime
and accumulated garbage of London as the Indian crew turned to
with powerful wash deck hoses and other cleaning materials, the ship
emerging some two days later as passably smart, her stone-coloured
upperworks washed down and her wooden boat deck sanded. More
attention to paint and polish detail would be given once fairer climes
were reached, but suffice it for the moment that a breath of fresh air
and spray of clean salt water brought respect back to the ship.

Watch-keeping was very quickly concluded as being a demanding business to the Cadet fraternity, not necessarily from the bridge duties point of view, but the awful need to adapt to a watch hours routine that never changed in its monotony. The 8–12 was reasonably civilised, allowing for unbroken night sleep, pre-lunch gins and an afternoon siesta. By awful contrast, the 12–4 did none of these things, whilst the 4–8 watch hovered somewhere between the two, in terms of impact. It was very quickly concluded therefore that the person with the best lifestyle was the Daywork Cadet, and once that conclusion was reached (it normally took about three days of watch-keeping), orders from the Chief Officer to revert to daywork routine were received with no small degree of relief. Pity the poor officers who had no such routine change to look forward to during sea passages, but as in all things, one became accustomed.

As *Cannanore*'s Third Officer so succinctly philosophised in his deep bass voice, 'Life at sea in cargo ships can be embraced quite pleasantly by big gins, big eats, big sleeps,' and as you might surmise from that, he stood the 8–12 watch, appreciated his pre-lunch gin, a large lunchtime curry and a sonorous two hours on his back from 2 p.m. to 4 p.m.

Cadets were not officially allowed spirits, but, and perhaps in contradiction with Indentures, two cans of beer per day were deemed as acceptable. Adherence to this really depended upon the goodwill of the Chief Steward, but as most Chief Stewards had a high tolerance level in most things, it was not unknown to exceed the allowed amount particularly when the P & O ships met up in port, and the social round was joined. Similarly, officers would occasionally invite Cadets to their cabins for time-honoured pre-lunch drinks, and it was by no means unknown for gin to be offered, if for no other reason than at 4/6 a bottle, it was cheaper than beer, just as long as the imbiber did not ask for tonic or somesuch expensive addition. Gin and water was the accepted tipple with perhaps Angostura bitters to complete to 'pink gin' aspect, and to ask for gin and tonic was a social blunder. At some 8/- per bottle, whisky was intolerably expensive; besides which, to drink Scotch before lunch was to display less than acceptable social grace, this being universally considered as an after-dinner drink.

Meals, as well as watches, became a daily regulator of routine on board the cargo ships, and were usually approached with great gusto.

P & O fed tolerably well, and with Goanese cooks and stewards, the quality of food and service was high, matched too by the covers. Mappin and Webb silverware was routine, with crisp white linen cloths and napkins, and silver service a matter of course. Afternoon tea was always served to officers' cabins rather than in the saloon, and even the Cadets were thus served by their Goanese steward, shared with the Fourth and Third Officers. Uniform was always worn in the saloon, and here perhaps the watch-keeping Cadets gained on their day-work counterpart who, thick with an admixture of red lead, wire grease and racing horse manure, had to scrub up and change out of working gear prior to eating – no concession was given to this save to those Duty Engineer Officers who were excused the use of the saloon to use the Engineers' Mess.

Sea fog, that most unpleasant entity for mariners, was another first experience for new Cadets, and was by no means unusual along the Portugese coast. During its duration, the Captain would stay on the bridge sometimes for as long as thirty hours with a consequent lowering of morale, goodwill and personal hygiene. A distant figure to Cadets at the best of times and one to be approached with great caution, the Captain became at these times a person to be treated with kid glove diplomacy and infinite attention, as an explosion was always imminent as the anxiety level heightened. Nerves were on edge, and whilst the Officer of the Watch had perforce to attend closely to the Captain's needs, it was prudent for the Watch Cadet to maintain a quiet, low profile as best could be achieved. It was not unusual for the Daywork Cadet to 'double' watches during such periods, and so it was on one such day. As eight bells were rung in the morning, so the day-worker bounded into the wheelhouse fresh from his shower, and with clean shirt and collar showing neatly white against the blue of his pressed uniform. His aftershave contrasted prettily with the stale atmosphere prevailing on the bridge, and he looked bright eyed through the bridge windows.

'Looks like it's clearing overhead, sir,' he chattered brightly, glancing back at the Officer of the Watch hunched over the radar.

Response came not from the OOW but from a grubby fawn dufflecoat surmounted by uniform cap with gold-braid across the peak that was propped against the starboard bridge wing dodger. In voice reflective of sleep lack, too many cigarettes and a general dislike for bright young Cadets, the Captain rasped, 'Fine, but we're not going that bloody way, are we?' and the ship's siren gave its mournful two minute dirge.

Mastering of the ship's 10 inch signalling lamp or the Aldis lamp was also part of the watch-keeping Cadet's duties, and the Third Officer took this function very seriously, no doubt partly in his responsibility for Cadet training.

'Call her up, bloke,' he would intone to his Cadet, pointing at yet another vessel approaching ahead (he actually called almost everyone 'bloke' which saved him the need to remember names) and off would come the canvas cover from the signalling lamp and visual morse would flash out – 'What ship and where bound?' – the standard enquiry then between merchant ships. Sending was relatively easy, but the halting reading of the response would often tax the patience of a bishop, to achieve an impatient, 'For Christ's sake, bloke, acknowledge, acknowledge.'

Matters usually got more fraught when the Royal Navy hove in sight, for their inquisitiveness appeared to know no bounds. Recognising that firstly it was not protocol for a P & O ship to challenge a RN vessel, and secondly that their bridge was liberally bestrewn with signalmen accustomed to signal at the speed of light, a low profile was usually adopted to the extent that everyone hoped she would not start the signals confrontation. Invariably the RN saw things differently, and no doubt recognising P & O vessels as almost family, they would challenge. The timing was often such that the standby Secunny (Quartermaster) had left the bridge to call the next watch and the watch Cadet had similarly departed to the poop deck at headlong speed in order to dip the ensign to her Majesty's vessel *en passant*, leaving the Officer of the Watch to handle a signalled exchange of pleasantries.

'Thank you, *Cannanore*, and bon voyage.'

Night time, of course, much reduced the ability to differentiate between Merchant and Royal, but the terse correctness of Royal Naval signallers was much preferred to the occasional severe error of judgement in calling up Dutch passenger vessels. The *Ruys* was all right, but the look of wide eyed horror on the Cadet's face halfway through trying to receive *Wilhelm van Oldebarneveldt* was a picture to observe, particularly as that always appeared to happen in the Red

Sea, when the OOW was too preoccupied avoiding other shipping to assist.

Gibraltar, seen for the first time through early morning haze, was as imposing as its reputation, and prepared by the Third Officer, a challenge from the signal station on Europa Point came as no surprise and was quickly answered.

'P & O vessel *Cannanore*, bound for Suez.'

As often as not would come in response a question – 'Do you wish to be reported to your owners?' That was the way in the fifties.

Onward therefore through the Mediterranean, patient Doxfords beating time in diesel tone, past Algeria and Tunisia, and between Sicily and Pantelleria to Malta, thence past Libya, finally to Port Said in Egypt, the western end of the Suez Canal, 1,900 miles from Gibraltar or six days' steaming.

It was inevitable that other P & O vessels were passed as they returned home towards England from Australia, the Far East or indeed India or Ceylon, and here was more of great interest to the new Cadets as protocol and tradition was unfolded before them. In essence, it was expected of the junior Captain to salute his senior by way of dipping his ensign, such salute being returned in a similar manner some moments later. Woe betide the Officer of the Watch who had failed to identify an approaching P & O vessel in sufficient time to have the ensign hoisted and manned for saluting, and indeed the vessel's name, such that relative seniority could be established. As Captains of cargo ships were invariably junior to those of passenger liners no such problem of seniority definition existed, and as *Cannanore* passed *Strathaird* protocol was properly observed in bunting. Each vessel had altered course to pass close to as was customary, and as flags dipped and ships' sirens bellowed across the dividing short stretch of water, so *Cannanore*'s complement heard clearly *Strathaird*'s public address system announcement from her navigation bridge. 'The black-hulled vessel we are now passing on the starboard side is the P & O cargo liner *Cannanore*, outward bound from London to Ceylon and India.' Unknown at the time to two of *Cannanore*'s Cadets, they had an appointment with *Strathaird* some two and a half years further along in their respective careers, unexpected in that as she no longer cruised, she normally carried no Cadets. However, that was later, and envious looks through binoculars at her white hull and romantic image had to suffice as each ship resumed her respective course and drew swiftly apart.

Cannanore also carried a few passengers, having accommodation for up to twelve in well appointed cabins on the deck above the dining saloon. Whilst rarely fully subscribed, the mode of travel offered was often preferred by those with the time to spare, or indeed a dislike for large passenger liners. A comfortable lounge with a small bar was about all the ship had to offer, other than sunbathing or leisurely reading on the boatdeck, which perhaps explained the rather hectic affair that developed on one voyage between the then Third Officer and a South American lady who had become quite affected by the ship's vibration and close proximity to all those sailors. Their closely guarded secret was held only by the entire ship's company, and his nocturnal clamber through her portside cabin window, having vacated the bridge to his 12-4 relieving officer, was observed only by the Second Officer, his Cadet and the standby Secunny of the Watch.

It was during the Mediterranean transit that rig of the day was changed from blue uniform to white tropical uniform, and the change signified that the voyage had really commenced. It also signified that many more laundry hours had to be embraced, as the white socks, shorts and shirts had an almost magnetic attraction toward cargo ship dirt, and moreover the complete lack of air-conditioning meant much perspiration had to be expected. Mr Errington's ministrations now came into their own, as articles of tropical clothing still in virgin condition were unpacked and tried on for the first time by those new to the sea, and not a few guffaws of laughter were heard as the shorts' length ended at knee level or below in true Pukka Sahib colonial tradition. Tailors in Calcutta and Madras would eventually fix that problem but it was present chagrin that needed address.

Laundry facilities consisted of a Bendix washing machine in the officers' 'heads', and an ironing board fixed to one bulkhead. The washing machine was of doubtful efficiency, or perhaps it was the washing powders of the day, but whatever the cause few managed to escape the agonies of 'dhobie itch' rash caused through the combination of high perspiration and inefficient rinsing, coupled to the need to use starch to keep shirts and shorts reasonably presentable.

'Rig of the day' change also meant that dressing for dinner had to be catered for, and it was standard practice throughout the P & O cargo fleet to change at 1800 hours into 'Red Sea' rig, which comprised a white uniform shirt with braid of rank on the shoulders (or in Cadets' case, on the shirt collar), long black uniform trousers, a black cummerbund, and black socks and shoes. It was, of course, a straight parallel with the Royal Navy and was often looked at askance by officers of other merchant companies in consequence. (In some years to come, when officers had to serve in the newly acquired P & O tanker fleet, the observance of the correct dress code became almost a fetish in a successful attempt not to become 'just another tanker operator', and gave rise to much amazement in such as Curaçao and other traditional tanker ports.) It was thus a dignified group of perspirants that would foregather for pre-dinner drinks, cooled only by the raucous punka-louvres, or whirring fans, that some were thoughtful enough to possess, and who would then file into the saloon as the melodic xylophone gong played through the alleyways, carried by a Goanese steward. It was the way.

Arrival at Port Said, and entry to the Suez Canal, was to enter yet another new world for the uninitiated, as the first noises and smells of the East were encountered. Some 87 miles long, two convoys of vessels passed daily through its length from west to east, whilst one per day passed east to west, their passing in the Canal facilitated then with by-passes off the main body of the Canal at Port Said, Ballah and Kahret in the Great Bitter Lake.

Seventy-six miles of the waterway were straight with the other eleven miles being curved, and night pilotage through these waters presented yet another task for the Cadets. Accustomed to working with the ship's carpenter during daywork duties, it now became necessary to assist him in manning the huge Suez Canal search-light housed in the forecastle head, enabled to its function of lighting the banks of the Canal simply by swinging back the 'gun port' sited in the stem, and so well disguised by the P & O emblem, the Rising Sun.

For watch-keeping Cadets, it was their function on the bridge to faithfully record every engine telegraph order in the Stations Book, and the passing of salient points for later and more formal notation in the ship's log. The Suez Canal Pilots were a self-portrayed elitist group of mainly British and French nationality who required constant pampering as to their food and drink needs, and this too kept the Cadets busy for the average of fifteen hours that it took to make the transit. It was both an exciting and an exasperating experience, with the cold night desert temperatures as counterpoint to the breathtaking dry heat of the day, and constant calls to 'stations' as the ship was moored or anchored to allow the westbound convoy through, or to facilitate the boarding, change or departure of Pilots. They left the ship inevitably clutching the bottle of whisky and 200 cigarettes so expected as 'gift' from the Captain. For all their hauteur, they were untouchingly human in their presumptions.

Some years later, when the British and French had left after the Eden Suez invasion, the *Chitral* (ex *Jadotville* of Compagnie Maritime Belgique) was similarly transiting the Canal eastwards but with a Russian Pilot, who on boarding had made it verbally very clear that he considered the British a boil on the bottom of humanity, and his time piloting *Chitral* a total insult. Word was quietly passed on the bridge that no sustenance of any kind would be offered to the man unless specific request was made, and that he was to be treated with aloof attention, but correctly. He sulked, and spoke never a word except helm or engine movement orders throughout his time aboard, leaving well on his way into a low calorie diet, distinctly huffy, and perhaps pondering the wisdom of his particular brand of diplomacy.

Departure from the Canal at Suez was viewed by all except the ship's carpenter with relief, because in his case night hours' attention to the Suez Canal searchlight and constant call to anchor or full 'stations' (his 'station' was on the forecastle, manning the anchor windlass) meant a rich haul of overtime payment.

Aden in South Yemen was the next destination, essentially for bunkering, a 1,300 mile voyage through the Gulf of Suez, the Red Sea and finally out through the bottleneck of Bab-el-Mandeb Strait into the Gulf of Aden, and the Arabian Sea. During these four days of steaming, Cadets would remain on bridge watch routine, as the sheer volume of shipping through these waters made this passage one to be treated with extreme alertness and fine attention to careful navigation. Radar usage was largely constrained as a means of position fixing by consequence of poor echo reflection from the low sandy shores and were not to be trusted. Navigational hazards as well as

potential collision situations were disproportionately high. It was a
period of extremely valuable experience for would-be officers.

There was the introduction, too, to yet another P & O myth, the
illusory existence of a 'P & O Buoy' moored in Position 18°00/N,
40°00/E (GP.Occ.F.Fl.), as a navigation mark for P & O vessels.
Some years later, the Orient Line also was allowed to utilise this
facility as a consequence of its full integration into the P & O family.

In 1957, on 22 October, the P & O cargo liner *Shillong* would fail
to make safe passage through these waters, colliding with a tanker
named *Purfina Congo* 190 miles south of Suez, still in the Gulf of
Suez. She sank, and one off duty Cadet, among others, went down
with her, the tanker having sliced into *Shillong*'s port side, reportedly
at about the position of the Cadet accommodation.

In a non-airconditioned vessel such as *Cannanore* the Red Sea can
be gaspingly hot with little relief, and four to a cabin at night
prompted means of escape to wider spaces with the illusion of relative
coolness. Engineers and Deck Officers alike became proficient at
making hammocks, and cabins were vacated for No. 4 hatch where
the hammocks were slung between nested derricks. The downside to
this was quickly apparent, manifesting itself in deposits of soot that
would rain gently upon the sleepers as the engine room watch 'blew
tubes'.

Off duty fashions changed too, with the Indian lungi becoming a
favourite mode of dress, to permit maximum air circulation.
Consumption of salt tablets became almost mandatory, particularly for
the Engineer Officers who had to contend with extreme temperatures in the engine room, and dhobi itch proliferated. An involuntary
cure was discovered by the first-trip Cadet who fell asleep whilst
sunbathing on the 'monkey island' (that strangely named upper
bridge deck) to find the next day that whilst suffering from severe
sunburn over parts that would not normally see the light of day, no
dhobi rash remained thereon.

The Great Dane took badly to these weather conditions, and the
Cadets found themselves as involuntary vets, but without the
necessary skills to do much more than to try to keep the gasping
animal cool as it lay as if pole-axed, under an improvised awning on
the poop deck. Occasional sandstorms that would whip across the sea
helped little in the quest for comfort, either canine or human, the

sand infiltrating everywhere with doors and cabin windows open throughout to attract the slightest breeze. Eventually, and having been brought to the Cadets' study to facilitate nursing, he finally, and with gasping pathos, died during passage between Aden and Colombo, being buried at sea, sewn into canvas coat by palm and needle, a sad application for the sail-making skills learned by the Cadets.

Strangely the horses seemed to suffer least to outward appearances, as they stood patiently in their boxes – as indeed they had stood from London, through the rain, the pitch and roll of the Bay of Biscay, and the gradual rise in temperature all through the Mediterranean to Suez. Theirs was to be an exhilarating gallop through the shallow waters of a Ceylon beach, with coat-tingling rolls in the sand to revive their spirits.

Aden, once *Cannanore* had been moored to buoys in the harbour by yet another British Pilot, was viewed askance, its still, hot dry air full of eastern babble, the harbour churned by small launches that dashed between ships and shore as surrogate taxis, or as in the case of P & O, as company business launches, brightly painted, brassware gleaming, and native crew in immaculate uniform as if the sun would never set on Empire. Even their boathook drill would have pleased many a Naval petty officer as they came alongside, to the trill of the Coxwain's whistle.

Aden – hot, dusty and barren, and famed for the bargains to be gained in purchase: all things electrical or transistorised, cameras, binoculars, silver and gold ware, clothing and shoes. Lighters, watches, and all manner of toys, with vacuum flasks, and insulated ice buckets were in great demand. All P & O vessels called in Aden, whether east or west bound, and the local economy benefited greatly when passengers from the white liners crowded ashore to purchase. Small naked boys in the harbour dived for coins tossed into the water by those too hot or uninterested for a run ashore, and amazed all by their twisting dexterity in the water. It was a service station that had opened an Aladdin's cave supermarket on its shores, and in that, surely, the first of its kind.

Cargo and mails were discharged to waiting lighters, and nudged ponderously away from *Cannanore*'s sides by smoke belching steam tugs, whilst bunkering was completed. A crisply white uniformed

Pilot boarded to be met by an equally crisp and whitely dressed Cadet to escort him to the bridge and the Captain. Officers and crew were called to stations for leaving harbour.

In the hot harsh sunlight, *Cannanore* let go from the buoys and proceeded to sea. Indian deck crew lined up in Naval fashion on forecastle and stern, their blue loose fitting uniforms allowing a bright contrast with the colourful cummerbund type waistbands and hat bindings of the Serang and Tindals. At signal from the bridge, the ensign was dipped by the Cadet on station aft to HM *Warship* at anchor near the entrance, and the shrill cry of the Naval Boatswain's Call fluttered across the water as the white ensign in turn saluted the red. That was the way, and *Cannanore* then set an easterly course towards Colombo, to the island of Ceylon that lay some 2,090 miles away, or almost seven days' steaming across the Arabian Sea and into the Indian Ocean. How one defines the boundaries between those two seas is a matter of no great concern, but presumably someone, somewhere, has charts that are appropriately marked such that war may be joined for territorial incursion.

After Socotra island, the next landmark would be the tiny island of Minikoy, and now for really the first time during the voyage, celestial navigation would become routinely necessary to fix the ship's position and guide her course changes. Cadets were stood down from bridge watches to 'get their hands dirty', albeit that their education was to continue under the watchful eyes of their officers, in practical sight taking with sextants, and the importance of getting the officer's sight correctly timed by the chronometer rather than misread by one or two minutes.

'Don't be one all your life, bloke, take a day off occasionally and get it right.'

The Senior Cadet probably remained as a watch keeper, thereby allowing the Chief Officer the luxury of reverting to day-work for the long ocean passage, the better to supervise his Serang and deck crew in the general husbandry of the vessel, and not least of all the Cadets in their appointed tasks.

Weather across the Arabian Sea was very much a function of monsoon activity and direction, and could be as pleasant as a Mediterranean summer, or as hot and soakingly humid as the inside of a Turkish bath with the added inconvenience of torrential rain and racing storms that lashed the seas into threatening heaps of ominous black. Ships and crew alike lurched and staggered their way through at these times, with little or no access for fresh air into the accommodation lest seawater followed, as green seas were taken aboard.

Flat aback on bunks or bed was the most comfortable way when off duty, wedged in with pillows, and so was it that particular day in the Cadets' cabin, with the upper and lower bunks furthest from the window (yes window, not porthole) occupied each by an off duty lad. The window had been cracked open about an inch from the top in an attempt to dispel some of the heat and moisture, but without too much positive effect, and life was at a low ebb. The lower bunk's occupant watched in amazement as a huge wave struck *Cannanore*'s port side adjacent to the cabin and a sheet of water, just one inch in thickness, flashed the width of the cabin from the window and dumped its several gallons squarely and completely on the Cadet above him. A chance in a million, as testified by the sounds of spluttering incredulity from above.

Not to become the independent Republic of Sri Lanka until 1972, Ceylon reflected strongly her colonial status in the fifties epitomised by her tea planter fraternity, the smart bush hats of Australian ilk for her police constabulary and literally hundreds of little Morris Minors that served as taxis in her capital city, Colombo. It was a green and pleasant island, peopled essentially by a gentle race although even then the spectre of language division, Sinhalese to Tamil, haunted the land. Colombo was and is the natural break point en route between East and West, and all of P & O's passenger liners called thereto for a brief few hours to say farewell to some and greet other passengers, as well as to load and discharge Royal Mail, some private cars, or small amounts of general cargo or tea. Their stopovers were timed in hours rather than days, and they would sweep majestically in through the harbour entrance, with flags flying, their decks crowded with passengers and their bridge with white uniformed officers. Huge anchors would flash into the water, and Colombo's large attendant tugs would fuss them to their ordained mooring buoys, while fleets of small launches would wait their moment to move alongside pontoons eased under their gangways, to carry passengers to excursions ashore.

For *Cannanore* and her sister ship *Coromandel*, the sisters *Devanha* and *Dongola*, *Kyber* and *Karmala*, and *Socotra*, those seven ships that comprised P & O's Indian cargo liner service, Colombo was a different matter in terms of length of stay. The speed and frustrations of handling their cargoes, inherent in the turbulent and chaotic unionised labour force, would invariably mean weeks there rather than days, and their officers would become accustomed to seeing such as *Arcadia* or *Iberia*, *Chusan*, *Stratheden* or *Strathnaver* depart for England, only to see them return to Colombo outward bound on the following voyage. That P & O's owners would fret and fume at the lost revenue potential was undoubtedly true, but far away from London, their officers and Cadets had to make the most of their incarceration, and so they did. Colombo was, in fact, rather a lovely place in which to be so incarcerated.

One particular discipline that pertained to P & O vessels in port, be they passenger or cargo (or indeed tankers in later years), was the observance of the flag ceremony at 0800 hours in the morning, when the ensign would be hoisted, and at sunset lowered, together with the Stem Jack, which was a diminutive of the Company house flag. The ceremony of 'colours' so called.

By Royal Naval tradition a 'preparative flag' would be hoisted five minutes before morning colours and hauled down at the appointed time. The hour was then struck on the ship's bell (eight bells) and the ensign hoisted. In the P & O a preparatory flag was not utilised, but it was the duty of the Watch Cadet to warn the Captain and Officer of the Watch that it was 'five minutes to colours, sir', or 'five minutes to sunset, sir.'

Again by Royal Naval tradition, when a vessel is in company, she takes her time from the Senior Officer's ship, and so it was with P & O. If a Naval vessel was in port, P & O would take her time, and when in port with a Company passenger vessel, the cargo ship would observe her time.

In Colombo, with the plethora of P & O liners and cargo ships calling, and the occasional presence of a RN vessel, it devolved upon the Watch Cadet of such long-stay occupants as P & O's India fleet to ascertain, by careful scrutiny of fleet lists, who was the Senior Captain present, and to follow his ship's lead. Woe betide him who got it wrong. It was not unusual to receive a signalled admonishment if a cargo ship of the fleet pre-empted a passenger vessel, or a vessel of the Royal Navy.

The liners of course went the whole hog with recorded buglers of the Royal Marines sounding the 'still' and 'carry on', and at sunset a full band of the Marines would sound out over the vessel's deck public address system. All good, stirring stuff. Some cargo ships would similarly upstage with recorded bugle and band records relayed through their bridge wing loudhailers but not when 'in company'. As a guest on board *Patonga* the Captain of a British India (BI) vessel berthed astern of *Patonga* observed her recorded 'Colours' ceremony. With a glass of gin in his hand, and literally tears in his eyes, he confessed to thank God that P & O was still upholding the traditions.

There is no record of the Commodore of the Fleet issuing 'order to the sentries of each ship to fire a volley of musketry at the hour of sunset'. The standard issue 'humane killer' pistol would not have been up to the task.

Colombo saw excursions to Kandy, visits to the Galle Face Hotel and countless diversions for *Cannanore*'s officers and cadets in their off-duty times. Her wardroom played host on several occasions to visiting officers from other P & O vessels, from other merchant ships and to the fairer sex from the Australian Embassy and local hospital. Cricket was also the order of many a day, and fixtures with ships of other Merchant Companies: Brocklebank, Clan Line, British India and more, were organised by touring through the harbour in the ship's lifeboat to whip up enthusiasm and games.

To say that Colombo was a waste of time was to express a corporate viewpoint – for Cadets, it was also opportunity to catch up on a neglected correspondence course, practise a few social graces, meet contemporaries in other companies and have the rare opportunity to visit the P & O liners in which they would hope, one day, to serve, here seen in fully fledged active foreign duty rather than in the deadly dirt and shabbiness of London's Royal Docks or Tilbury.

All good things came to pass, and *Cannanore* eventually sailed from Colombo for her ports of call in India, namely Madras, Vishakhapatnam and Calcutta; although in retrospect the sequence of call is hazy, the squalor that prevailed in each is not, particularly Calcutta. Articles of cotton uniform were cheaply available in Madras and much sought after, whilst Thursday was a 'dry' day in terms of obtaining beer at the Mission for Seamen or Flying Angel Club. Sex could be obtained behind the slag heaps at Vizag for the price of a bar of soap (or so were informed the incredulous Cadets who as one declined the opportunity) and a breathless climb to the Buddhist monastery up many hundreds of steps (or so it seemed) ended in an embarrassing refusal to meet the extraordinary financial demands of greeting monks, or however they styled themselves.

Arrival to the mouth of the river Hoogli and the subsequent river passage to Calcutta's docks was, however, different. In the words of some unknown philosopher, who may or may not have been a P & O Captain, 'Bombay is the gateway to India, the Hoogli river is the arse, and Calcutta is ninety miles up it.'

In the approaches to and upward through the Hoogli, the Captain insisted that a Cadet man 'the chains', a wooden platform that protruded over the ship's side, from where he, the Cadet, could heave the lead to report to the Bridge the depth of water prevailing. The art of 'heaving the lead' had been instructed at *Conway* and no doubt at other nautical colleges, but the reality in practice was something different in a moving vessel.

To achieve the greatest distance ahead of the chains, it is necessary to swing the 10/14 lbs lead on its line overhead in a circle two or three times before casting it forward. Successful on several soundings, 'by the mark five, sir' and so forth, familiarity caused contempt, and showmanship developed — swiftly abandoned as the lead, carelessly this time put into its upward arc, stopped at the overhead zenith and plunged downward towards the Cadet's unprotected head. Only swift footwork and an awkward body angle prevented a nasty accident as the lead whipped past his ear, to be abruptly halted a foot above the coffee waters of the Hoogli, the lead line snapping taut round his neck. High embarrassment, a lively ropeburn round the neck, and only slightly mollified by roars of laughter from the Bridge.

The slow push up the Hoogli, its waters not much different in colour from the sewage that it carried from Calcutta, was an experience never to be forgotten in its many aspects. Country craft, piled so high with what appeared to be reeds that they resembled floating haystacks (reedstacks?) were a regular feature, and the general flotsam that passed the vessel was considerable in its variety, and certainly included dead animals, their bloated bodies rafts for the evil

13. *Outward Bound – character building through adventure. Would-be P & O Cadets Stern (extreme left) and Perry (crouched)*

14. *King George V and Royal Albert Docks, London early 1950s*

15. King George V and Royal Albert Docks, London, early 2000s: London City Airport

16. *s.s. Cannanore, deployed in the Indian trade-lane 1950s*

17. Cadet Davie, starboard bridge wing. s.s. Cannanore *1956*

18. Cadets Perry, Davie and Paston, ashore in Colombo 1956

19. Andaman Islands, working timber from jungle to Cannanore*'s holds*

20. Wardroom of s.s. Rajula *(British India Company) entertains officers of* P & O, Cannanore, Madras

21. Christmas aboard Shillong *at sea, 1956*

22. s.s. Shillong, *deployed in the Far East trade*

23. Cricket in Penang

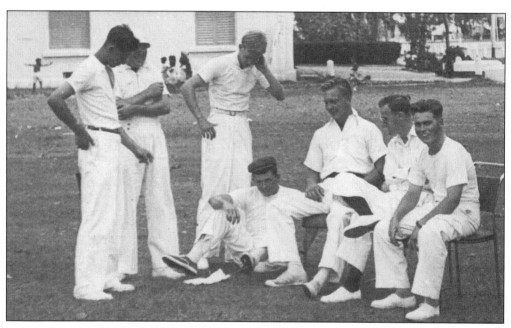

24. Shillong *vs* Pinjarra *1957. Cadets Marsland, Whillance, Bishop, Tavender, Perry, Ferguson*

black birds that rode them downstream. Human carcasses too spun and swirled downriver, the crows paying them no less attention than their companion animal corpses.

Night hours in the Hoogli meant careful watch to be maintained on the foredeck where the wire and rope hawsers were laid out ready for mooring in Calcutta, for it was by no means unusual for local craft to creep stealthily alongside under the overhang of the bow, their presence masked by the thud of the ship's engines and noise of her passage through the water. Once there, their occupants would slip aboard, their bodies black and greased, to pass the ship's ropes down through the hawsepipe, never to be seen again.

Seamanship, too, was at a premium here, for as the Hoogli was a bore river, it necessitated far heavier mooring capability in the river berths of Calcutta than would suffice alone with wire ropes or manila hawsers. One of the ship's two anchors had to be 'hung off', to free the anchor cable for such mooring purposes, a daunting task whilst under weigh, but one of immense interest and value for Cadets under training as this was one of the few opportunities to observe and be involved in such a task. That examiners of Masters and Mates never asked how such an operation was handled, but rather insisted on questioning how sheerlegs would be rigged over the engine room skylight whilst at sea, is a matter of historical fact, and the source of some irritation to P & O Cadets who had been there, in the real world rather than that of idle unlikelihood.

'Sheerlegs, sir? Simply dismantle three 5-ton derricks from No. 4 hatch, instruct the Serang to spirit them to the engine room skylight, and reassemble them in sheerleg configuration.'

Routine everyday stuff, as the Merchant Navy all over the world weekly practised drawing a main engine cylinder whilst hove to in a force 9 gale.

The arrival to Calcutta river berths was a fussy and frustrating business, with the need for careful manoeuvre to secure the cumbersome anchor cable to the huge river buoys, followed by wire and rope hawsers ashore. Exasperated almost beyond his patience by the heat and noise of *Cannanore*'s engine room and what was even to the Bridge Officers the finickity lack of competence of the Pilot, the Welsh Second Engineer gave vent to his wrath over the telephone, with the timely reminder that *Cannanore* was a diesel ship.

'You've got three more engine movements, two blasts on the whistle, and then you're on your bloody own!' he roared over the telephone.

Calcutta was a mess: hot, humid, indescribably dirty and with a peculiar odour of its own somewhere between that of a mangrove swamp and a farmyard. Progress along the main road of Charingi was to press through a cast of thousands in perpetual stink of perspiration, diesel fumes belched forth from ramshackle hand-me-downs from London Transport, and carbon monoxide from the seemingly hundreds of Sikh driven taxicabs, all of doubtful vintage. Coupled to all this was the noise, as each driver demonstrated his total belief that his vehicle was propelled by horn power alone. And the betelnut juice! One of India's less attractive contributions to mankind, betelnut was sold at every street corner, wrapped in green leaves and flavoured to taste before being shoved into the mouth to chew, its juices apparently conducive to peace of mind, being an intoxicant of a kind. The need to rid the mouth of a build-up in saliva was continuous and spurts of excess juice shot from behind the reddened teeth of almost every pedestrian, or so it seemed to the incredulous eyes of one's first encounter. Pavements, walls, everything, even poor old *Cannanore*'s decks, were liberally spattered. Cows wandered aimlessly through the traffic, secure in the sacredness of their being, opening their bladders and bowels at random. Humans, observing the call of nature, would stand or squat as necessitated and perform, any personal embarrassment long ago subjugated by the impossibility of an alternative. Inhabitants lived and died on the pavements.

The taxi ride from city centre to the ship's berth was another lesson learned. Never take a taxi when travelling alone if the driver carries a co-driver. Twenty minutes of directionless driving into the dark streets of Calcutta's night were followed by confrontation with the two bearded Sikhs, ugly and threatening in their demands for money far in excess of a taxi fare. More than a little frightened, one paid. Bike-shaws were slower, less dignified, but with not too many bicycles made for two, the odds were much improved.

The necessity to have yellow fever injections in Calcutta brought about further and more personal exposure to matters of locally practised hygiene; for the fourteen or so officers from *Cannanore* that required the jab, the doctor unbelievably used the same needle for everyone, without so much as a hint of sterilisation between arms. One Cadet, last in the line, watched horrified as his turn approached, and as the needle left his arm, so he gave a great shudder and fainted clear away.

Talk of medical personnel brings sad memories too: memories of those Anglo-Indian nurses that would arrive on board for the dance in the Wardroom (the so called Che-Che Ball) desperately trying to identify with the Western world, their sing-song Indian accents clearly not from the valleys of Wales as they would have you believe. Beautiful, many of them, belonging to neither Britain nor India, and at that time, accepted by neither.

The absolute highlight of the vessel's call to Calcutta, however, was the arrival on board for breakfast of no less a personage than the Chairman of the P & O Company, Sir William Currie, and much time had been spent to ensure that *Cannanore* gleamed for the occasion. His boarding was greeted by the trill of the Boatswain's Call, much practised over recent days by the Serang and two Tindals. The Captain and his Senior Officers, immaculate in freshly laundered and pressed tropical uniforms, were at the gangway brow to salute him aboard.

Some two hours later, a telephone call to the Cadets' quarters advised the Senior Cadet to have one of the 'Chota Sahibs' muster at the head of the gangway to salute Sir William ashore, and he who drew the short straw hurried thereto. The Captain, Chief Engineer and Sir William appeared from the accommodation door that gave access to the maindeck, and walked briskly as a group towards the gangway, where now stood at rigid attention the Junior Cadet with his guard and band of Serang and two Tindals in close support.

Renowned for his interest in personnel, Sir William acknowledged the salute afforded him, and pausing before the astonished Cadet said, 'Thank you and good morning. Tell me. How is HMS *Conway* these days?' Obviously Sir William as Chairman did more homework in personnel management than his Deputy Chairman, Sir Donald. To great effect.

Madras, by comparison to Calcutta, was a relief, with less of the oppressive atmosphere that pervaded the latter. Presumably the local population cooked over fires fuelled by dried buffalo dung as in Calcutta, but the evening breeze direct off the Bay of Bengal seemed better able to dispel the accumulated odours and smoke, and of course Madras suffered not from the extraordinary overcrowding of the capital city of West Bengal.

It was famous for an availability of inexpensive tropical uniform items, however, and it was here that such as S.W. Silver and Company of Eastcheap lost out in sales to their subcontinent counterparts, as supplies of long white cotton stockings, cotton shorts and shirts were ordered, the shorts and shirts being turned out at extraordinary speed and low cost despite being made to measure. The quality was good too, and guaranteed to withstand the rigours of non-air-conditioned wear, constant drubbing by single programme Bendix machines and the doubtful gentleness of Company issue soap powder.

Madras was also to experience meeting with that grand old lady of the British India Line passenger fleet, the *Rajula*, which plied her trade between India's east coast and Malaya as was, carrying what seemed an extraordinary number of 'deck passengers'. In 1957 she still had some seventeen years of BI service remaining, but at the age then of thirty years, she plodded with quiet dignity at her sedate 12 knots about her business, the Third Officer reportedly being paid a penny per head of passengers carried to organise the distribution of drinking water *en voyage*.

To the impressionable young Cadets, *Rajula* was an eye-opener. BI was part of the P & O group, and was therefore looked upon somewhat as a 'country cousin', but in this part of the world, there was no doubt as to which vessel held peacock position. Permanently stationed in India, with her mostly British officers on 'foreign service', there was an atmosphere prevailing on board that smacked of freedom from Head Office interference, manifesting itself on the Bridge in the shape of many potted plants and shrubs, not quite a usual sight in P & O passenger liners. There was also the playing of 'trains', by her officers, demonstrated from their cabins situated along the boat deck.

This game was briefly but succinctly demonstrated to *Cannanore's* startled officers as they were entertained aboard *Rajula*. Doors to the officers' cabins with their wooden jalousie slatting and windows that lowered into the lower door, opened directly onto the open deck and looked, in their continuity along the deck, for all the world like a railway carriage. At a blast on a whistle, half a dozen cabin occupants walked to their respective doors, opened them as one, entered, slammed them closed as one, to lean out of the window space and wave farewell. 'Stand clear of the doors please,' and with another toot on the whistle, the 'Orient Express' departed. Slightly zany fun, its madness partly encouraged by the function of being 'permanently on station'.

The Wardroom of *Rajula*, blessedly unaffected by whatever rules the Indian local State Government might impose, entertained *Cannanore*'s officers liberally, and much perspiring good humour was found in her dark panelled surrounds, grouped round a venerable upright piano with lusty singing accompanied by a BI officer on fiddle, and two from P & O with guitars. *Cannanore*'s Senior Cadet, his indentures finished halfway through that particular voyage, was in fine, flushed voice, himself in happy limbo between Chota and Sahib. He was enjoying the transition.

Voyage followed voyage in not dissimilar fashion on the Indian run, but noteworthy deviations from what was seen as normal sometimes occurred, and such was the case with a visit after a Madras call to Port Blair, in the Andaman Islands, that group of islands situated in the Bay of Bengal. Port Blair, described then as 'a lonely outpost of the Indian Empire', and situated on the eastern side of South Andaman was where *Cannanore* dropped anchor, to prepare herself to load several thousand tons of huge hardwood timber, floated out to the vessel in large rafts, each log not less than 5 to 7 tons in weight, and many much more.

As always, the Wardroom sought distraction away from the often oven-like heat of the ship's environment, and although India was known to have swung a cricket bat from time to time, the tropical denseness of jungle surrounding Port Blair, crowding greenly down to beach heads of glistening white sand, scarcely indicated that the noble game had made much inroad or headway here. Swimming over-side, whilst looking provocatively cooling, was dissuaded by the obvious presence of watersnakes and a reported quantity of lurking sharks, and even the Second Officer's apparent attempt to make the *Guinness Book of Records* for venereal achievement seemed short of contribution here.

P & O's Agent in Port Blair was up to the challenge, however, and to the delight of those off-duty, arrangements were made to transport a group by tender (shades of the *African Queen* only slightly larger) to the area where the timber was firstly felled, and then worked by elephants through the jungle to the sea, for eventual enrafting to the waiting ship.

Whilst the intricacies of snatching heavy awkward logs into the wings of *Cannanore*'s holds were infinitely interesting to her Cadets, the ride through jungle on the back of an elephant, as the beast physically worked the timber with tusk and feet to the mudslide loading to a river, was unique and unforgettable. Memorable also were the hairs on an elephant's back, comparable to porcupine quills. The subsequent curry lunch served in a palm frond hut raised on stilts from the sands of that tropical beach, with even the drinking water tasting of curry, was stunningly different.

The Fourth Officer, in the absence of cricket, took away one of the ship's motor lifeboats, suitably stocked with cold beer and sandwiches, and with a group of some ten stalwarts, puttered off towards a likely looking river entrance, intent upon exploring up-river. His continued absence for several hours thereafter brought the Captain to a boil of anxiety, having been belatedly informed by the Agent that such a trip was without wisdom, as a tribe of head hunters was known to be active still in the area. Safely return they did, however, although the Captain's process of coming off the boil produced a chastened but unrepentant Fourth Officer, who had hugely enjoyed his Humphrey Bogart casting for that part of the day.

One near mishap occurred when another group used the same lifeboat for a small fishing expedition, the sudden snatched arrival into the boat of a young shark almost prompting precipitate departure from the boat of occupants, as violent avoiding action ensued. A prompt and vicious swing to the beast's head on the part of a hammer-swinging Chinese fitter saved the day, but further incident with the boat, when three of the Cadets went exploring a small adjacent island, finally ensured the confining of boats to their davit stows. Once again the font of belated information, the Agent had informed the Captain that the innocuous looking island now alive with cavorting Cadets was known locally as Cobra Island, in view of the prolific number of cobras resident thereon! In thankful retrospect, none had been sighted.

South-west to Colombo, north-west to Aden and then the Red Sea. Homeward bound. Well, almost, save for the quick call into Port Sudan with yet more new experiences for first time visitors. Breathtakingly hot, it was awe-inspiring to watch local desert tribesmen, attracted toward temporary employment in the port, hump huge sacks of gum arabic or groundnuts with apparent ease, rhythmic movements encouraged by their own strange sounding vocal dirge: 'fuzzy-wuzzies', originally called so by apprehensive British soldiery, because of their hairstyle, wildly matted and fixed in position by an admixture of fat and camel dung (first trip Cadets believe almost anything) and pinned by large wooden combs. It was easy to understand at close proximity how Tommy's apprehension turned to fear when faced by hordes of such men, hate-filled and intent on killing. Here though, they were content to smile and poke incomprehensible fun at the young Cadets sent to supervise their cargo handling and stowage, and to steal a little when opportunity arose.

Port Sudan had its sporting distraction too, a challenge from a ship of another company to play at water polo. Nothing loath, the languid Third Officer led his team forward to victory although the effort of playing this particular aquatic game in what amounted to a hot, highly saline bath was deeply depleting. The subsequent night cargo watch passed in a dehydrated daze, caring little for what Fuzzy-wuzzy was up to in the cargo holds.

The Captain brought his vessel back again to London, and watched with his usual wry amusement as the Shore Superintendent clucked and fussed about, shouting unnecessary instructions to the Bridge and mooring parties, demonstrative of his apparent surprise that the vessel could be navigated over vast distances and into strange ports without his actual assistance.

November 1955 to October 1956 and not one of *Cannanore*'s Cadets had been selected to join the cruise liners during the summer Mediterranean cruising season.

However, changes were afoot and Mr Errington was able to advise certain of them that they should expect a directive from Head Office in Leadenhall Street to proceed on long leave, with new appointment to follow. Never wrong, word was indeed received to that effect, and for one, a whole month of leave ensued, awaiting new orders.

CHAPTER 11

The Far East Run: *Shillong*

T HE *SHILLONG*, BUILT IN 1949 as was the *Cannanore*, was however some 30 feet longer than the latter, some five feet beamier and with a larger cargo lifting capacity. Her steam turbines also made a faster vessel, and indeed with her rakish length and slim black funnel she looked every inch more active than *Cannanore*, and somehow well suited to her trade lane of employment, the Far East, where she served in tandem with her sisters the *Surat*, the *Singapore*, the *Sunda*, *Somali* and *Soudan*. The 'S' boats, so referred.

Shillong, however, was not a happy ship in the sense that *Cannanore* had been, and she seemed moreover accident prone. That is not to say that good times were not had aboard, but the nervous disposition of the Captain seemed only to bring about a state of semi-permanent 'What's going to happen next' throughout the vessel, and perform-ance was like that of a highly strung racehorse in consequence. Officers of the Third and Second ranking, whilst adequate at their job, had an alarming interest in alcohol when in port, and often consequent irrational behaviour. The Third Officer, although not falling into that category, was such a pompous and incompetent ass as to cause equal despair to the Cadets appointed to the vessel, and to the tender guidance of these officers. Thus was it an unhappy ship, and to her came one of *Cannanore*'s Cadets and indeed *Cannanore*'s Carpenter, a Petty Officer of considerable dedication to his job, and an unusual crouched, but competent, approach to use of the cricket bat! These two were actually destined to sail in several P & O vessels together, to include the liners, but their cricketing association was to cease after *Shillong*'s matches in Penang.

The joining of *Shillong* was to hear that the appointment thereto was to replace another Cadet around whose legs the anchor cable had whipped when a joining shackle sheered at anchoring in a Japanese port the previous voyage. With severe multiple fractures to both legs, it was only the skill of Japanese medical attention that had saved the lad's legs, and P & O had spared no expense in flying him home for final attention by one of Britain's leading bone surgeons. The memory of that moment proved too much for the Captain during the coastal voyage that preceded the deep-sea run, as a shrill screamed instruction from the Bridge to 'clear the area forward of the compressors' inevitably came from his throat prior to the order to 'let go the anchor'.

Shillong was also the ship in which London's dockers gave another lesson to the over-confident, but this time in theft. Bolstered by some ten months of sea-going experience, one of *Shillong*'s newly joined Cadets was acting in his anti-pilferage role, being present in one of the designated 'spirit lockers' as hundreds of cases of whisky, gin and beer were loaded for various discharge ports in the Far East. Nothing passed his eagle eye, and it was quite obvious just who had won this particular round in the continued battle to prove to London's dockers that attractive items of cargo were not theirs by divine right.

Cloth-capped, friendly and smiling, the six-foot docker approached the Cadet and offered his congratulations on the way the Cadet was doing his duty.

'All's fair though, mate, 'ow'd you like to see 'ow quick I can open a case of booze, take art a bottle and reseal the case so's you'd not spot the loss?'

Wisely his offer was declined, but not to be put off, the offer of demonstration was earnestly repeated, with the firm promise that the bottle once removed from the case would be similarly replaced, with no chance of theft.

'Purely for demonstration purpose, mate, you see.'

In the interests of science the demonstration was agreed, and with immediate and deft manipulation of the wooden case and its wire binding, indeed within ten seconds there stood a bottle of whisky on the lock-up's steel floor, with the case to all appearances untouched. Testing the strength of purpose before him, the docker queried the bottle's return to its box, but the Cadet was firm. True to his word, with a twist of his cargo hook and a shove here and there, the docker replaced the bottle with not even a scratch on the wood to mark its passage in or out.

'You're too smart for me, mate,' chuckled the man of magic, and sauntered back to his work, the stacking of cases arriving into the ship, with his gang.

Several weeks later, at destination discharge, four empty whisky cases were found behind the stacked goods and to add injury to insult, two dozen empty beer bottles languished in their opened cardboard cartons having been casually consumed in London to keep throats various free from dust!

Shillong's passage to the Far East mirrored that of the *Cannanore* as far as Colombo in Ceylon only, but thereafter she turned only slightly north of east to make toward landfall on the northern tip of Sumatra, prior to passage through the Strait of Malacca (no Greek name that!) to Singapore, a distance of some 1,600 miles.

The voyage to Colombo from Aden had, however, been made through the relatively clement weather of the start to the north-east monsoon. This coupled to the Chief Officer's intent not to have his Cadets seen as lazy watch-keepers, saw them 'turned to' each day as day workers, and their hours were spent crouched over screaming, noisy, air-driven (or was it steam) deck scaling machines, as they strove to meet his daily allocation of steel deck to be scaled and thereafter red-leaded for weather protection, and finally painted.

Prickly heat was now augmented by the stinging shower of rust particles, and eyes filled with perspiration behind protective goggles. Sunburned necks were rasped by the sticky wetness of denim work shirts, and uniform caps were replaced by an assortment of headgear, protection against the overhead sun. These ranged from beaten up old panamas to the Mrs Mop appearance of one Cadet who sported a white cap-cover (once white cap-cover) to match his once white shorts. There was no more welcome sight than the palm trees of Ceylon, indicative of a return to watch keeping and the relative comfort of uniform.

Long extended port times were not as regular a feature for P & O cargo ships on the Far East run as for those bound to India, but time enough there always was for social activity ashore and on board, and the usual sight of the large liners arriving and departing with much ceremony and bustle.

The planned holding of a dance in the Wardroom was put down by the Captain (somewhat petulantly it was thought) because of reported trouble with police aboard *Coromandel* during a recent and similar such occasion. Nothing loath, arrangements were nevertheless made for the venue to be established ashore, at the residence of some from the Australian consulate. The snag was that *Shillong* was to provide the liquid refreshment, the removal of which from the harbour area was forbidden.

It was thus that on the appointed evening, a group of P & O Officers and Cadets, immaculately attired in uniform caps and full Red Sea evening rig, sauntered casually toward the dock gate most adjacent to *Shillong*'s berth, there to take a small fleet of Morris Minor taxis to the intended venue. That their officer-like bearing and formal uniform dress impressed those members of the Ceylon Constabulary on duty at the gate was indeed fortunate. Hanging down inside each trouser leg of the approaching group was a bottle of spirits, suspended by string attached beneath the wearers' cummerbunds, their walk not so much the result of days at sea, but rather the intricate need to move forward within the constraints placed about their lower limbs.

His potential promotion unseen, the Police Corporal saluted the group as they passed through the gate, although surely he must have wondered at the physical condition of these men as they eased their strange way into the awaiting Morris Minors.

The party was an unqualified success, although congratulations heaped upon one Cadet the following morning back on board were most puzzling to the recipient, to say the least. He was finally horrified to learn that a proposal of marriage to one of the Australian girls at the party had been accepted! The pretence was successfully maintained until just prior to departure from Colombo several days later, and was the cause of much concern and worry to the young Lothario. Another move along the learning curve.

So from Colombo towards Singapore, but first a call to Penang, the visit there marked by the meeting with another P & O cargo ship, the *Pinjarra*, an occasion for a cricket fixture between the two vessels, and much inter-ship fraternising between officers and Cadets. It was a grand meeting and completely typified the *esprit-de-corps* that existed within the P & O in those days.

The younger brother of *Cannanore*'s Third Officer was very much in evidence batting against *Shillong*'s team as a Cadet serving in *Pinjarra*, as was the wild colonial boy from Ireland, to be met again soon as a fellow Cadet in *Iberia*. That was a little later though, and Penang's cricket was only interrupted for the occasional 'refreshment' over, and the somewhat startling arrival of the Chinese kite flyers onto the pitch, as an unusual but interesting distraction. *Shillong's* Fourth Officer, an extraordinary entry to P & O's officer ranks by way of the Queen's Sword at Royal Air Force College Cranwell and subsequent endeavours after Squadron service, brought necessary grace to après-cricket sundowners, and in a large part compensated for the lack of social involvement from the Second and Third Officer rankings of *Shillong's* complement. The game's result is forgotten, the playing not.

Through the Malacca Straits to Singapore, and here one of *Shillong's* passengers disembarked, a woman who had suffered severe privation at the hands of the Japanese in Changi jail and whose completely white hair for one so relatively young bore mute testimony to the fact, although her calm philosophy belied it. Her invitation to the Cadets to lunch at her residence one day was accepted with alacrity as a rare moment of privilege, although her after lunch insistence that they should, siesta style, rest in a darkened room whilst she too rested in her room came as an unusual but not unpleasant experience in the afternoon steaming humidity of Singapore.

One of the unfortunate differences that existed between the Royal Navy and the Merchant, and that to include the P & O, was that sea going staff of the Merchant Navy rarely socialised with shore staff, and that was particularly obvious in such places as Singapore and Hong Kong, where the P & O (and probably others) had expatriate staff appointed to management posts, to look after fleet and business interests. No doubt some social contact existed at the Captains' level, but a very clear gulf separated sea from shore personnel, in odious comparison to the comraderie that so clearly existed within the 'Fleet List'. So it was that with duty hours done on board, distraction ashore was left to those who sought it as best they could. Over the years, contacts were to develop which would make each main port call a pleasure of anticipation, as old acquaintances were renewed, with dinners and cocktail parties away from the vessel a relief from normal shipboard routine.

Some years later and berthed in Singapore on the *Chitral*, the Third Officer was preparing to dine ashore to the invitation of the local Director of the Metal Box Company. Dressed in tropical suit, he took his black rolled umbrella from its stand to protect from the sudden gusts of monsoon rain that at that time of the year plunged with dumping wet suddenness from leaden overcast skies. His Chinese steward, entering the cabin and taking swift appraisal of the situation, handed the officer the little used briefcase that gathered dust in a corner.

'Now you go ashore like proper English gentleman,' he solemnly intoned, and scurried laughingly away to rejoin his Mahjong school.

However, that was to come, and suffice it to say that the Singapore Swimming Club and Manley Road Swimming Club saw much of the off-duty Cadets as they flopped thankfully into the relative coolness of pool waters, relief from the pervading heat and stifling humidity that was Singapore.

There was amused distraction too at the Tanglin Club, that most elite of rendezvous, at the sight of British Army Officers (they all appeared to be portly Majors) with their ballooning khaki shorts that reached over the knees to meet the uprise of khaki-stockinged legs.

There was the first taste of oysters at the famous Tanglin Inn Restaurant, and a conviction ever thereafter that oysters are an over rated pastime.

The awed but distanced view of Raffles Hotel was somewhat degraded by the tipsy cries for help emanating from an adjacent monsoon ditch into which the Second Officer had fallen, and the sticky heat of purchases in Change Alley.

Singapore's cricket ground, her teeming bikeshaws and the surprising juxtaposition of Chinese with Malays and Indians that comprised the population, was a source of constant interest to new arrivals. An interesting commentary on that society was to be heard in later years from a Chinese resident who when questioned as to the melding of such diverse indigenous groups, was to reply somewhat cynically that if confronted simultaneously by an Indian and a cobra, he would first step on the Indian. Actually voiced, but surely not true.

Under the guidance and advice of the always immaculately uniformed Singapore pilot, renowned for his colonial pomposity, *Shillong*, her duties discharged, eased her sleek black hull away from Singapore, and turned east of north through the junk-infested waters of the South China Sea towards Hong Kong, some 1,430 nautical miles steaming.

Shortly thereafter her Cadets once again resumed their 'day-work' duties to their now total disgust. It was surprising how attitudes

change, but for some three to five days at sea, not too much could
be achieved in terms of large scale projects, which usually for that
Chief Officer meant large scaling of decks. Instead, and with amazing
lack of forethought, his Cadets were instructed to strip and varnish
the gangway rails, surprising in the light of the dripping humidity that
prevailed. Discouraging as the conditions were, the task was
achieved, as evidenced by the sticky handed first ascent of the
gangway in Hong Kong by whichever unfortunate, most likely a
Customs Officer. Another lesson in seamanship learned, at the cost
to P & O of several tins of good varnish.

These would, in all probability, have been replaced by a ships'
chandler in Hong Kong (along with many other items of deck stores)
at a profit that reflected both in his girth and the unmarked envelope
that would slip in familiar Hong Kong fashion into the Chief Officer's
'Office'. Chief Officers were no different from those of other
companies in that vulnerable regard, although it is fair to say that their
baksheesh was by no means as substantial as that of Chief Stewards! It
was nevertheless there from ships' chandlers particularly, or con-
tractors when husbanding work was undertaken by shore gangs on
board. Hong Kong too was a favourite spot for the sale of ship's old
wires and hawsers that had reached the end of their useful life,
although Cadets new to the experience found it puzzling that it was
not unknown for brand new manila hawsers supplied in London by
a caring P & O, to be sold in Hong Kong as 'old'.

Temptation here was real, and whispered information from black
clad Chinese to incredulous, impressionable and impoverished Cadets
that large sums of money could be achieved by selling cases of whisky
from the cargo lock-ups prompted planning as to how this could be
achieved. The risks were of course enormous, and the penalty for
such direct contravention of Indentures too severe to contemplate.
Notwithstanding, *Shillong*'s Cadets, completely convinced by the
honeyed tones of their would-be Chinese benefactor, put plan into
action one dark night as the ship's officers loudly and brightly
entertained selected guests to a dance in the Wardroom. Access to the
hold and 'specials' locker was of course easy, as necessary keys were
quickly obtainable from the Chief Officer's office. The removal and
subsequent transfer to the ship's main deck, via the hatch ladder, of
two cases of Johnny Walker was however less simple, the task made

no easier by the 'Red Sea rig' of the two Cadets involved, themselves temporarily absent from the wardroom festivities. Achieved it was though, and at a pre-arranged signal, out of the penumbra that shadowed *Shillong*'s outboard side glided a black painted small watercraft, its passage through the harbour's dark waters skilfully and silently achieved by a single scull oar.

With relative riches shortly and easily to be theirs, conscience prompted by background and training rushed forward as 'Jiminy Cricket', and the two Cadets eyed each other silently. Both from first class pre-sea Colleges, they silently acknowledged without further ado that whilst the excitement of planning and execution had been adrenalin stimulating, to finally hand over the loot would amount to common theft, and despite the angry and frustrated threats that were hissed at them from the waiting boat, they ordered the Chinese connection to push off. The whisky was, with further puffing and grunting, returned to the lock-up and the two Cadets to the Wardroom party, no longer guilty by intent or achievement, and enormously relieved in consequence.

They were to sail again together, and indeed work together in later years in a shore capacity, and there is no doubt that each would have carried a deep regret forever had the contemplated sale taken place. The hissed threats of severe bodily injury from their intended Chinese purchaser certainly kept the excitement on the boil for the remainder of the Hong Kong call!

More harmless distractions there were in Hong Kong, though, to include cheerful evenings at the Mess of the Army Teaching Corps in MacDonald Road, halfway to the fabled Peak where on one Chinese New Year, small cracker balls were laughingly and somewhat tipsily cast from the mess windows onto unsuspecting passers-by below. Repercussions would later be heard in Shanghai!

A rickshaw race through the night streets of Kowloon was another event that evolved. No doubt prompted by high spirits and spurred by a passing Tiger beer, it was to the utter amazement of the two Chinese coolies that they found themselves passengers in their own rickshaws, observing the young, sweating and over-indulged white Caucasians between the lurching shafts of their respective means of livelihood. The unseemly but highly satisfactory gallop ended up outside the doors of a much publicised brothel, but once again mindful of Indenture wording the two Cadets allowed themselves to be hauled back, unsullied, to the Star Ferry, rickshaw coolies once more in command of their vehicles, albeit casting the occasional apprehensive glance backwards at their laughing passengers, who continued to view the occasion as a re-run of *Ben Hur*.

Jimmy's Kitchen; the Star Ferry; the cable car to the Peak; made to measure shoes, shirts and suits; junks; Aberdeen's floating fish restaurant and the sheer pulsating beat of Hong Kong's enormously populated being made a never-to-be-forgotten impression; as indeed did the peculiar achievement of one member of P & O's Agency staff, which was to collect soapstone models of miniature couples, carefully handcarved to posterity in positions of sexual embrace anything but missionary. Doubtless he achieved other things as well, but nothing, surely, as noteworthy!!

Hong Kong would be revisited many a time in the *Canton*, *Chitral*, *Arcadia* and other P & O liners, but for Cadets the P & O cargo ships were largely their only access to such exotica, and appointment to vessels on the Far East run were therefore much sought after.

On departure from Hong Kong, *Shillong* turned to the north-east, to steam through the Strait separating Formosa, later to be Taiwan, from the Chinese mainland. Taiwan was to become the last sad, ignomious and undignified graveyard for such as *Chusan* (1973), *Orcades* (1973), *Himalaya* (1974), *Oronsay* (1975), *Iberia* (1972), *Arcadia* (1979), and *Orsova* (1974) to mention just some that went down to the scrap breakers' hammers, but that was not to be known as *Shillong* passed Kaohsiung on her starboard beam, en route to Kobe and Yokohama on the Japanese island of Honshu.

Hong Kong and Japan saw Cadets spending much of their in port watch-keeping duties down below in the hatches, and in particular the 'specials' lockers that housed wines and spirits outbound, and the 'attractive' items produced in the Far East for export to Europe. They were there as a deterrent to theft or pilferage as well as to ensure proper stowage in conformity with the Chief or Second Officer's cargo planning, and time spent below was usually unpleasantly hot and dirty, and often boring.

In Kobe, one such duty became alarming as the Cadet was approached by the squat but powerfully built figure of a Japanese docker brandishing his cargo hook in menacing fashion. He stopped in front of the Cadet and gazed at him silently, perspiration trickling down his bare torso and soaking into the straining waistband of his discoloured shorts. Suddenly, raising both hands swiftly and sharply above his head he screamed 'Hiroshima, boom!' and accusation shone hotly from his narrow eyes.

'N-nothing to do with me, bloke,' the Cadet stuttered, and beat a hurried retreat up the hatch access ladder, to hoots of derisive laughter from behind him.

Japan meant different things to different people, and for the Captain it was to relive his previous voyage's nightmare of a Cadet flung to the steel deck like a rag doll by the shuddering whip of rogue cable chain, and the agonised screams that followed. Each time an anchor was dropped or heaved up, his high-pitched warning cries keened from bridge to forecastle, ironically to 'stand clear of the spurling pipes', and the Third Officer with his attendant Cadet would dutifully muster upon Jim the stalwart Carpenter, at his station behind the windlass.

To the Chief Officer it was to give reluctant shore leave to his eagerly anticipatory Cadets, with stern admonishment as to the venereal perils that lay in wait in the multitude of bars and Japanese steam baths that flourished ashore. That two of his young charges reported back on board for day-work at day-break, their boiler suits hastily drawn over shore-going mufti (one had mysteriously mislaid his underclothes) was cause for a display of angry reprimand and later punishing allocations of yet more deck plates to scale as penance.

Thankfully, the Third Officer had no need, in his role as ship's Medical Officer, to administer penicillin in pursuit of cure. One Cadet left Kobe squeaky clean and positively drained of energy having attended three steam baths in one afternoon, his back almost broken by the tramping feet of the attendant masseuse. All in all, Japan did not represent the most cultural of experiences for *Shillong*'s Cadets, but that in part was due to the somewhat pedestrian approach of most of her officers, who unfortunately had little interest outside a somewhat narrow, studied combination of grain and juniper berry.

One result of the extra punitive deck scaling imposed on the two erstwhile Cadets would have well enhanced the image of P & O in the eyes of other Merchant companies, and indeed the Board of Trade examiners had any question been directed as to deck plate maintenance.

'Well, boy, how would you approach the preparation of deck plates after scaling and before the application of top coat protective paint, given that you have limited time before pre-dinner pour-outs?'

'Eh, well sir, by treating the scaled area with red lead.'

'Exactly, but how would the application be made, given a wide range of brushes?'

'Well, sir, we have found by experience that to up-end the drum of red lead onto the deck gives immediate material to work with, and fast coverage is gained by the judicious usage of two rubber squeegees, which being useless for wash down purposes thereafter, are quietly committed to the sea.'

Fortunately or unfortunately, the method was not revealed, and the tackiness of the deck area for days thereafter was put down to humid ambient conditions.

Arrival to the Pilot Station at 0500 hours in the mouth of the Yangtze Kiang river, en route for Shanghai, was an eye-opener in more ways than one for the uninitiated. Chinese militia with their red-starred fur hats and machine guns at the ready repaired quickly on board *Shillong* and dispersed rapidly to commanding positions throughout the vessel. The Commissar and his staff took over the main saloon, and commenced with great suspicion and precision to scan through discharge books of all personnel on board, provided by the Chief Steward on sharp and imperious demand.

All hands were mustered, and under the searching gaze of the Commissar, were forced to file one by one through the saloon, to receive a keen comparison between documented photographs and the real thing. All cabins were searched to ensure that no one avoided the muster, and the atmosphere to say the least was tense. Two of *Shillong*'s Cadets were also Midshipmen Royal Naval Reserve, and whilst this was not reflected in the available papers, a casual request by Royal Naval personnel in Hong Kong to 'keep your eyes open, lads, for things that might be of interest to us,' sub-consciously heightened their tension, lest they be singled out for particular attention.

Passage to Shanghai was therefore somewhat red-eyed, as perhaps suited the political atmosphere, with militia unfriendly and possessive in their continued watchful and unwelcome presence.

Shore leave was not allowed, and the stay in Shanghai was marked by that most unusual of concerts, twenty-four hours of non-stop classical music boomed forth from loudspeakers placed up and down the cargo wharfs, surely an achievement never matched or even attempted by the Port of London Authority in their struggle to retain or gain business.

Ever keen to demonstrate P & O's social side, *Shillong*'s officers also, whilst somewhat bemused by their sudden arrival on board, entertained right royally officers from a Russian freighter berthed close to. They watched fascinated as their visitors quaffed their way through copious amounts of British spirits and smoked their strange cigarettes that apparently required the filter to be squeezed two ways between finger and thumb before the smoking could take place. They left the ship with protestations of eternal friendship and apparently unaffected by their intake, which could be described generously as generous.

Shillong's Radio Officer also left the ship, although his departure was swift and unfriendly in the event. Over-enthusiastically recalling the events at the Army Teachers' Mess in Hong Kong, and retaining in his cabin some cracker balls left over from Chinese New Year, he flicked one laughingly through the open window of his cabin during a pre-dinner 'pour-out'. The unfortunate result was that it landed right behind the Chinese guard stationed at the bottom of the ship's gangway. The loud and unexpected 'crack' of its explosion prompted, on the part of the soldier, immediate loss of composure, possibly a little water, and considerable 'face' to the effect that after a quick rush of adrenalin, feet and irate guards, the Radio Officer was hustled ashore to wherever recalcitrant wrong-doers were then hustled in Shanghai. His return to the *Shillong* was only eventually achieved, some few days later, after the Captain had written a personal letter of apology to the Chinese People's Republic, and the Radio Officer had been subjected to much mental stress by misinformation that his ship had sailed from Shanghai without him.

The voyage home to London was for the *Shillong* surprisingly uneventful, and for her Cadets an admixture of watch-keeping duties, correspondence course and day-work. There was, however, a flavour of anticipation too, for she was due to arrive in London in late April. That meant that with the P & O Mediterranean cruising season due to commence in May, the opportunity potentially existed for appointment to a cruise liner, and much time was taken up in debate as to who would achieve such an appointment.

Iberia and *Arcadia* would both be cruising that year, and each would receive a complement of some eight Cadets to man the ships' launches used to ferry passengers ashore at certain cruise ports. The phenomenon known throughout the British Merchant Service as 'the Channels', that feeling of heightening excitement and anticipation after months en voyage, was therefore further stimulated for the Cadets as Ushant was rounded, and course set north-easterly through the Channel towards the Thames and home.

Speculation was rife as to whether Mr Errington would know on arrival at the Royal Docks, for such was his reputation, and final arrival thereto was laced with apprehension accordingly. Even the dirt and smell of King George V docks failed to dispel some anticipatory excitement. True to form, one of the P & O 'choice Pilot' White twins brought *Shillong* from the locks, 'Sun' tugs belched their fumes as they jostled and strained at his whistled signals, and the Shore Superintendent oozed open disbelief in the ability of the ship to manoeuvre alongside without his fussy intervention. (In *Shillong*'s case, he probably had a point!) Customs Officers boarded, and went unerringly to the iced water jug of the Second Officer where once again the contents had amazingly turned to neat gin ('Do you wish to pay duty on this, sir, or shall we pour it down the sink?'), and *Shillong*'s main engines fell silent, their function temporarily complete.

One Engineer Officer, purchaser of some considerable yardage of silk for his fiancée's wedding dress, learned that HM Customs have a heart, but he almost missed it, as he denied a perceived slur on the value of his careful purchase.

'What would you say is its worth, sir?' he was questioned, the Boarding Officer hefting the obviously large bolt of silk in his hands, 'perhaps five pounds?'

'Certainly not,' hotly rejoined the declarer, 'that's real silk that is,' but before he could bring all to naught, the Customs Officer smoothly intervened.

'I'll ask you again, Sir, about five pounds?' and he looked meaningfully at the Engineer Officer.

Light dawned, and suddenly aware that officialdom was rooting for him, he agreed in grateful tone.

'Ah, ah yes, about five pounds would be it,' he confirmed, and was rewarded accordingly with the confirmation that 'in that case, sir, no duty will apply.'

With Customs clearance formalities completed and the shore gangway in final position to the satisfaction of the Shore Superintendent, Mr Errington of S.W. Silver and Co. boarded, his appearance in the Cadets' cabin eagerly awaited in the knowledge that his information as to new appointments would precede the somewhat pedestrian passage of orders through official channels. Ever aware of his position, and always careful not to raise hopes falsely, his words were nevertheless heard as gospel, and time proven as accurate.

To two of *Shillong*'s Cadets, he brought great cheer, and as he sipped his Allsopps beer thoughtfully provided from hoarded supplies, he confirmed in his own inimitable fashion that service in *Shillong* was thankfully at a close.

Precisely six months later, on 22 October 1957, the tanker *Purfina Congo* sliced through *Shillong*'s port side adjacent to the Cadets' accommodation. *Shillong* later sank with the loss of one Cadet, the Chief Steward and several racehorses. The news of the collision came as a great shock, but to many, no great surprise.

'I believe, gentlemen, that whilst you will be proceeding on leave of absence, it would be prudent to consider the purchase of white tropical uniform and mess kit for your next appointments, in preparation for the cruising season. I am aware,' and he coughed discreetly, 'that foreign suppliers may have provided white uniform shorts and shirts during your recent voyages, but be sure that you are adequately stocked, bearing in mind the travails of boat work.'

His words were music to the ears, but in the purchased event, horrifically expensive, for the P & O gave absolutely no financial assistance toward such hefty purchases. In that, the second year of apprenticeship to the P & O, the Company paid to Cadets the princely sum of £150 for the full twelve months of service, and it is factual that most by circumstance had to involve a 'tailors' bill'. In a sense, they were beholden to the Company store, unless of private income status, which admittedly some were. To kit up for a cruising season on a P & O liner would see little change from £100 in 1957, even assuming that blue mess kit was not purchased (Cadets were allowed to utilise normal 'day' uniform with wing collar and bow tie for evening dress), or that replacement of everyday uniform was not necessary to liner standards. Notwithstanding, appointment to the liners was what P & O was all about, and scant thought was given to the cost. To this, Mr Errington was quietly grateful, and the P & O complacent.

A cursory glance at uniform items required by a P & O Cadet for cruising would read as follows, as a minimum:

Uniform Cap & Company badge	1	
No. 1 blue uniform	1	
*No I blue mess – kit	1	(optional)
Uniform white shirts	3	
Uniform black tie	1	
Uniform black shoes	1	(pair)
Uniform black socks	4	(pairs)
White boiler suit	1	
White cap covers	1	
*No. 10 white uniform	3	(plus brass button set)
*No. 10 white mess jacket	3	(plus brass button set)
*No. 10 dress shirts	2	
Cummerbund	1	
*Bow tie	1	
Uniform white shoes	1	(canvas or buckskin)
*Uniform white socks	4	(short)
Uniform white shorts	4	
Uniform white shirts	3	(tropical)
Uniform white socks	4	(long)
Cadets' patches of rank	1	(pair)

Those asterisked would be purchases specific for passenger liners, but bearing in mind the standards of dress that were required aboard the P & O liners, an absolute minimum of purchase that rarely sufficed the actual demand.

As in many other ways, the P & O Officers' white tropical uniform for passenger vessels was unique to the P & O, and in this was an unusual departure from the Royal Navy whose standards were usually espoused by the line.

The Royal Navy 'No. 10' white tropical uniform jacket is worn over the vest, and sports a high closed collar that clips together under the chin, often referred to as a 'choker 10' jacket. The Orient Line, later taken over by the P & O, affected similar style.

By contrast P & O Officers wore the usual white shirt and black tie, the white uniform jacket to all intents and purposes being worn as a single breasted item of clothing with four brass buttons bearing the P & O rising sun emblem. It was surprisingly practical compared to the 'choker 10' option, allowing easy discard of the jacket on the bridge when passengers were not around, or indeed for Purser Officers in the Bureau (or Ship's Office) when going about routine duties.

Extract from P & O Regulations, reprint dated 31 October 1956

Discipline – Uniform
The Company's uniform is to be worn by all Officers when on duty on board their ships. The regulation for uniform is laid down in Appendix A.

Appendix 'A' Uniform
The uniform to be worn by Officers in the service of P & O S.N. Co. All ranks, when on passage in the Company's steamers, are to wear uniform if the Commander considers it necessary to do so.

Coat	Blue Cloth, Navy Pattern, double breasted, four Company's buttons.
Distinctive marks (Cadets)	Vertical stripe of Russian gold braid forming notched hole, with small Company's button at the upper end, worn on each end of collar
Cap	Navy pattern, black mohair band, 1½ inches wide; gold anchor on band, and Company's badge above.
Vest	Single breasted, blue cloth with six small Company's buttons.
Trousers	Navy blue cloth or drill, according to climate.
Mess jacket and waistcoat	As worn in the Royal Navy, but with Company's buttons and distinctive marks.

White clothing	The jacket to have a turn down collar with a white shirt, collar and tie. Shorts will not be worn, but the wearing of shorts in cargo ships is left to the discretion of the Commander.
Overcoat	As worn in the Royal Navy, but the Company's buttons and distinctive marks.
Tie	Black silk.

CHAPTER 12

Mediterranean Cruising: *Iberia*

T HE APPOINTMENT OF CADETS to certain of the P & O liners for the summer cruising seasons was a matter of expediency, as many of the ports visited were unable to accept these large vessels alongside. This required that the ship anchored off at a safe but reasonable distance, thereafter to ferry her passengers ashore to their various excursions or sightseeing in the ship's launches.

Trained at pre-sea Colleges to proficiency in handling of relatively small boats, the Cadets' presence 'in command' was almost always reassuring to the holidaymakers embarked between ship and shore. The naval precision that P & O insisted upon, with Indian crew members at bow and stern in their singularly individual uniforms and practised boat hook drill, only enhanced the feeling of 'Britishness', and indeed flavoured the general cruising atmosphere with that touch of 'Raj' that was so much part of the P & O.

To say 'almost always reassuring' is true, because despite training, Cadets in their youthful exuberance were occasionally known to be less than reassuring at times in the handling of their boats, or indeed passengers, at moments of stress or tension. On balance, however, they handled their duties professionally and in some cases with much fortitude in the face of passenger tantrums, which very often surfaced in the heat of the day, or indeed in distress at having to sit close to the diesel engine, in the confines of the 'limousine's' midship's cabin.

However, that was all unknown to the eight Cadets, selected from cargo ships various of the fleet, who received official confirmation of appointment to the big ships. Their orders from Leadenhall Street were to join s.s. *Iberia* in Tilbury Docks – not King George V, not Albert Dock but Tilbury, homebase of the liners at that time. If whoops of glee were heard from Eastbourne, St Johns Wood, Ireland, Pinner, Chingford and Bombay (Bombay?), then it was to recognise that the joining of P & O had finally and really come to pass, despite the cost of more uniform.

The boys of *Conway, Worcester,* Warsash and Pangbourne or at least some of them, had made it! 'They were going cruising!!'

Tilbury Docks, some few miles downriver in the Thames from the Royal (so called) group of docks, were really only distinguished from their upriver counterpart by their then added inconvenience of access and the fact that they catered largely for passenger ships, the inconvenience factor only alleviated as far as passengers were concerned by rail connection. The same turgid Thames flowed past and filled her dock area, and the smell was largely similar. Dock labour tramped as dirtily through the liners as the cargo ships in the 'Royals', but with more facility to bespoil ships' facilities.

The liners in consequence sat squat and belittled by their surrounds, unmajestic in their imposed captivity, but frantic in their efforts to look good, look majestic, for those that had chosen to pay for their services.

Painters painted, and Green and Silley Weirs, offshoot of P & O, green and slimed their way up and down engine room ladders to bring repairs to main and auxiliary power plant, and much dirt and confusion to present to Engineer Officers returning from leave to take their engines to sea.

Cleaners, upholsterers, curtain makers and carpet fitters, launderers and suppliers various, all combined to take P & O to the cleaners, whilst on the bridge, engineers from Decca, Marconi and electronic people various, strove to bring navigating systems firstly to work, and then to perfection.

Board of Trade officials inspected lifeboats and life saving devices, and examined lifeboat classes comprising Stewards and other odd crew members in the waters alongside the ships, intent on instilling some degree of competence into those that perforce might be called upon to save lives in the event of collision or grounding, and knowledge of the boats that might be used.

Stores were delivered, and signed for to the fiscal advantage of Shore Chief Stewards who grew fatter from the proceeds (those breasts of chicken always seemed to turn out as wings and legs) and Kelvin Hughes delivered charts appropriate to Mediterranean cruising and so ordered by the Navigator, or Second Officer in the P & O.

To this bustle, this pre-cruise bustle, came the eight Cadets, and having seen the passenger liners sweep in and out of Colombo,

Fremantle, Hong Kong, Sydney, and places various in their sea-going splendour, they may have been excused the initial gulp of dismay at that which they first saw crouched in Tilbury, awaiting release to the clear sea.

Built by Harland & Wolf of Belfast, and launched in 1954, *Iberia*'s 719 feet of length and 31 feet of beam were layered by many decks of accommodation and facilities, and surmounted by a huge buff coloured funnel situated at mid-length of the vessel and back from the Navigating Bridge. She looked immense to those that came from the foot-soldiery of the P & O fleet, the cargo ships, and indeed her gross tonnage of 29,614 tons was further weighty evidence of a change in league. A thin wisp of grey smoke from her funnel proved that at least auxiliary life existed aboard, and that the ant-like activity up and down her gangways and through the stores 'gunports' offered noisy and real proof that despite her look of moribund resignation, life was far from at an end. Far, far from it, because *Iberia* was going cruising!

In this, some 113 years later, she was to perpetuate the name into the Mediterranean, for it was thereto that her namesake had steamed in the August of 1844, the first *Iberia* of the P & O, as announced in the *Illustrated London News* of 20 June 1844.

A six weeks tour by steam to Athens, Smyrna and Constantinople, calling at Gibraltar and Malta, with the option of visiting en route Vigo, Opporto, Lisbon, Cadiz and Gibraltar. The Peninsular and Oriental Steam Navigation Company's well known splendid steam-ship *Iberia* will start from Blackwall on Monday August 5th for the above ports. Time occupied in the passage out and home about six weeks. Very superior accommodation for passengers. The *Tagus* will follow the *Iberia* on the 25th August. For terms apply at the Company's offices, 51 St. Mary Axe, London.

That particular *Iberia* was a wooden paddle steamer built at Limehaven in 1836, of 516 gross tons! She carried no Cadets!

For the cruising season, *Iberia*'s Cadets would be quartered in the First Class passenger accommodation on 'D' deck, in four of the two-berth cabins situated immediately outside the First Class Restaurant.

That this was a cause of no small anxiety to the Chief Officer is probably true, as it meant that some seven decks separated them from his watchful eye, their off-duty activities largely disciplined by constant threat of surprise audit visits.

It was also a source of potential dismay to two of the cabin stewards, for whom a cruising season would normally represent huge leaps in gratuities received from grateful passengers, and largely undeclared for tax purposes. Cadets represented no such potential income, being largely impoverished by their £150 annual apprentice payment, need to purchase uniform and to observe a lifestyle as befitted a Cadet of the P & O.

As it happened, one such steward chose to let his frustration show forth in surly achievement of minimum attention to his two cabins involved, whereas the other, older, wiser and a Master Mason to boot, tucked his four young gentlemen (as he insisted in addressing them) firmly into his care, and acted in surrogate avuncular fashion for the rest of the three month cruising season.

He was 'Biff' Kemp, Master Mason, Petty Officer RN (rtd), Cabin Steward and always welcome guest to pre-meal 'pour-outs' in his young gentlemen's cabins. In his early sixties, and with a stomach indicative of some years of attention to hop products, he would nevertheless, when asked to demonstrate, draw in his belly and solemnly bend over to touch the carpeted deck with palms of hands outstretched before unbent legs, a feat achievable by few of his young audience. He would sometimes perform the trick without being asked, but that would indicate that a few beverages had been consumed in his 'peak' prior to coming on duty. His admonishment at the sight of a Cadet pouring beer incorrectly into a glass was always Royal Navy in delivery style, as he pulled his shoulders back in his medal be-ribboned white jacket.

'Angle of 45 degrees, sir, angle of 45 degrees!' he would roar, then smile contentedly as his instructions were hastily obeyed.

When Masonic meetings were held on board, he would always attend, strangely not out of place in his Steward's uniform among the dinner jackets and mess dress of passengers, and those ship's Officers that belonged to the order. 'Good evening, Master Kemp,' he was respectfully addressed by the Purser, and so it was.

Boating, however, was their *raison d'être*, and it was to the boats that the Cadets, now clad in snow-white boiler suits and uniform caps, turned their attention in order to familiarise themselves with the handling abilities of the craft available.

Iberia, as did her sister *Arcadia*, carried six power boats that were utilised to carry passengers ashore to excursions, four 'limousines' (so-called) and two 'penny-buses' (so-called). Whilst all six were of similar size and carrying capacity (circa 70 people) the four 'limousines' were custom built for the task, looking quite sleek in their lines, with a midship and forward cabin as well as open air seating. The small 'bridge' situated just aft of the cabin contained wheel, gear/throttle control and revolution counter and it was from here that the Cadet in charge would cox his craft, capable of some 12 knots speed and highly manoeuvrable.

By contrast, the 'penny-buses' were little more than standard lifeboat in appearance, with no cabin or awnings for protection from the sun, or indeed occasional rain. Rather than the utilitarian bridge position of the 'limos', the 'PBs' sported a rather mundane metal steering wheel that adorned the after end of a small radio shack, and instead of the synchronised gear throttle of the 'limos', a separate gear stick and throttle lever. Their plodding knots of speed were appropriate to their more homely appearance, and whilst they were far harder to manoeuvre, they were comfortingly safer in any sort of a seaway, as testified during *Arcadia*'s cruise season a year later. More of that later, however. The 'limousines' would cut a dash, but the experience of sitting in their enclosed midship cabin next to the throbbing, powerful and heat/fume producing diesel engine would cause many a passenger to seek later passage in the clean Mediterranean air and sunlight afforded by the 'penny-buses'.

Tilbury Docks, therefore, became a boating lake as *Iberia*'s Cadets practised their craft and rid their system of a natural urge to come alongside the ship's narrow gangway platform in a flurry of speed and flying spray, Spitfire-like in the daring of the manoeuvre; rather, to remember that passengers preferred the more stolid approach that would not cause their summer clothing to be soaked by the sudden whoosh of water wedged skywards between boat and gangway, or indeed the sickening crash of boat against gangway as the manoeuvre misfired. By and large, and by the time that *Iberia* put to sea for the first cruise, the Chief Officer was able to anticipate with some hope that, barring a small disaster, P & O's passengers would be safe in the now practised hands of his young coxswains. Almost always, they were.

Other boat work also took place during the work-up to the start of the cruise season, with involved Surveyors of the Board of Trade examining those crew members that had studied for their Lifeboat Certificates, to ensure that they were properly versed in the handling of standard lifeboats, and were able to assume authoritative control of such a boat in the event of an abandon-ship situation.

Cadets, already possessors of the Certificate, and well experienced in boats, were set to assist on occasion, and so was it on one particular day.

The Steward assigned as coxswain during his test displayed strong effeminate genes and seemed happier with hand on hip rather than tiller, but nevertheless made a determined effort to demonstrate his ability and grasp of the correct nautical terminology. He successfully had his crew toss oars, and then bring them to the rowing position secure in the rowlocks. The order to 'give way together' would have seen him through the test, and that particular P & O lifeboat surging through Tilbury's mucky waters, but his actual instruction to stalwart crew to 'bear down together' brought only a pregnant pause followed by unrestrained laughter. He was nevertheless a very good Steward, as were many of his kind that sought and found refuge in the P & O liners of those days. As lifeboatmen – well, perhaps.

The *Iberia*, one of the largest liners on the Australian run at that time (the other was her sister ship *Arcadia*) had a passenger capacity of around 1,390: 655 First Class passengers and 735 Tourist Class. Although it has been said that *Arcadia* was the more popular of the two, certainly the cruise programme of *Iberia* that season was most satisfactorily subscribed, and seen through the eyes of her Cadets, well and truly enjoyed by her passengers, determined as they were to make the most of their holiday. For the Cadets, it was an extraordinary experience, no longer available with the passing of that era and the consequent change in the approach to cruising. It was savoured to the full.

In June 1957, *Iberia* left the confines of Tilbury Docks, piloted therefrom by the P & O 'choice' Pilot, and with Captain Pollitt (later Commodore) in command, proceeded, once more majestic, toward the Mediterranean, sun and fun.

Passengers were mustered at their boat-stations, and the intricacy of their cumbersome cork life-jackets explained over the ship's public

address system as Officers and Cadets moved among them to give
more personal instruction or reassurance, as and when necessary.
Stern warnings were given as to the danger of throwing cigarette ends
over the ship's side (always use the sand-boxes distributed throughout
the public decks) and the foolhardiness of sitting on the ship's rail.

For the next three months she would trace and retrace her tracks
between the UK and ports of call various in the Canaries and
Mediterranean (and indeed one cruise to Hamilton, Bermuda), and
names synonymous then as now with a cruising itinerary reeled off
the Navigator's charts one by one, some just once, some to be
repeated on another cruise. Gibraltar, Tenerife, Palma, Malaga,
Naples, Lisbon, Las Palmas, Madeira, Vigo, Cannes, Kos, Dubrovnik
and Venice.

For these same three months, her Cadets would work and play
hard, savouring to the full the golden opportunity, and the unaccustomed life aboard one of P & O's then largest liners.

If they had thought of the Captain of a cargo ship as awe-inspiring,
then he that commanded *Iberia* took on a God-like position in their
eyes, as distant from them as could possibly be by reason of his rank
and responsibility. God-fearing himself, he would preach ardently at
Sunday Church Services at sea (compulsory attendance by all Cadets,
and why not?), and perhaps somewhat ironically, often about the evils
of sex. His strong beliefs were reflected also in his membership of the
General Council of Missions to Seamen. Tall, slim, with grey bushy
eyebrows surmounting a strong aquiline face and always immaculately
uniformed, he was the epitome of what was anticipated of a P & O
Captain. Indeed, in October 1957, he was appointed Commodore of
the P & O fleet.

As part of their training aboard, Cadets undertook various
functions on the Bridge as *Iberia* entered or departed a port. For three
of them, the Bridge therefore was their 'station': one to attend the
two large brass handled telegraphs to the engine room, one to write
up the station's log (or Bell Book, sometimes referred) and one to act
as general dogsbody, usually accompanying a Quartermaster hoisting
or lowering flags as appropriate.

Coming from the relative smallness of a cargo ship, *Iberia*'s Bridge
appeared immense, the number of personnel in attendance at
'stations' constituting a positive crowd scene. The Captain would

mark the Pilot to ensure no errors of judgement would rebound upon his head, and the Staff-Captain was always there, presumably in case the Captain suffered illness or worse. Similarly, the Chief Officer to more effectively control lowering of gangways, boats and so forth. The Officer of the Watch would mark the Captain, intend on catching every order, which he would then repeat to the Junior Officer of the Watch who hovered around the telegraphs and phones to relay such orders. Three Cadets and three Quartermasters made up the complement to a usual total of twelve persons, except when such as the Purser or Surgeon was invited to the Bridge. Oh, and not to forget the Indian seamen, usually two in number. No wonder that cargo ships incarcerated in Colombo had been so impressed by the display of uniforms and gold braid on the bridges of the liners as they swept in and out.

As *Iberia* edged cautiously into the harbour waters of Tenerife, the Spanish Pilot demonstrated his agility of movement, if nothing else, by racing from bridge wing to bridge wing, as he issued his pilotage instructions. The Captain was exasperated and hard-put to keep up, and the scene was rapidly turning to farcical proportions, as helm and engine movement orders were showered forth, passed on, and repeated back to give assurance of compliance.

'Hard a port, slow astern starboard'	– Pilot
'Hard a port, slow astern starboard'	– Captain
'Hard a port, slow astern starboard'	– OOW
'Hard a port, slow astern starboard'	– JOOW
'Hard a port, Sir' (confirmation)	– Quartermaster
'Slow astern starboard, Sir' (confirmation)	– Cadet
'Hard a port, slow astern starboard it is, Sir' (complete confirmation)	– JOOW
'Hard a port, slow astern starboard it is, Sir' (further confirmation)	– OOW
'Aye, Aye' (acknowledgement)	– Captain
'*Gracias*, mid-ships, full astern'	– Pilot
'Midships, full astern'	– OOW
'Midships, full astern'	– JOOW
'Midships, Sir (confirmation)	– Quartermaster
'Full astern, Sir' (confirmation)	– Cadet

25. *s.s.* Iberia *cruising 1957*

26. *s.s. Iberia cruising 1957. Back row: Goddard, Johns, Lucas, Peartree, Harrington. Front row: Harvey, Ferguson, Davie, Perry*

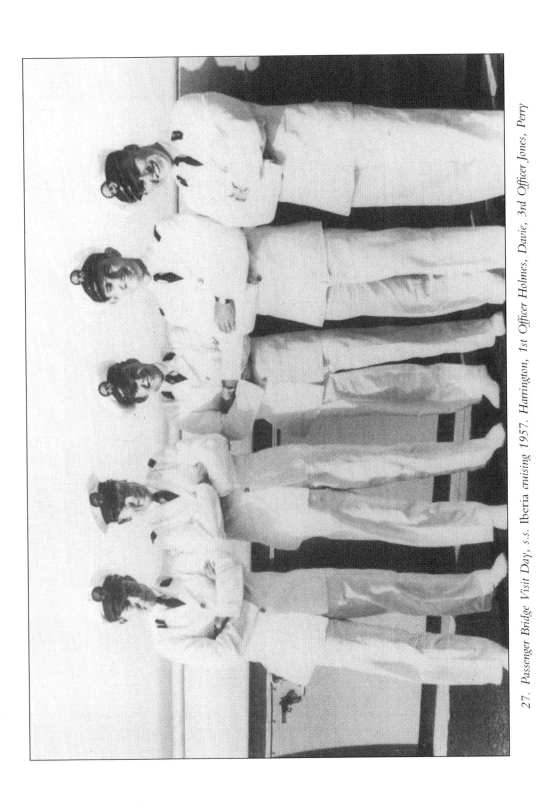

27. *Passenger Bridge Visit Day, s.s. Iberia cruising 1957. Harrington, 1st Officer Holmes, Davie, 3rd Officer Jones, Perry*

28. s.s. Iberia *cruising 1957*

29. 'Limousine' launch service for passengers

P. & O. S.S.   **IBERIA**

QUIS NOS SEPARABIT

The Cadets of the 'Iberia' request the pleasure

of the company of

....

at a Cocktail Party in the Wardroom

on Sunday, 1st. September, at 6.15 p.m.

CARRIAGES AT 7.15 P.M.   DRESS FORMAL

30. Invitation to cocktail party

31. Cadets' Cabin Steward 'Bif' Kemp, Master Mason, Petty Officer RN (Rtd.) – all round good bloke.
'Angle of 45°, Sir, angle of 45°!'

32. Iberia *1957, 1st Class Dining Room (Gala Night). Davie, Perry, Ferguson, Harvey*

33. Arcadia *1958, 1st Class Dining Room (Gala Night) Falkner, Senior, Porteous, Lane, Perry, Willi*

34. Arcadia – back on the Australian service

35. *Wardroom, s.s. Arcadia, cruising 1958. Back row: Willi, Porteous, Falkner. Front row: Senior, Lane, Perry*

and the Cadet tending the telegraphs dutifully pulled the two brass handles of the portside telegraph to the 'full astern' position.

To his amazement, they slipped back to the 'half astern' position, and reacting swiftly to this apparent mechanical fault, he restored them to the ordered 'full astern' position.

Horrified now as they yet again moved, independent of his hands, back to 'half astern', he grasped the handles firmly to find that they now resisted his strength. Swiftly he glanced in semi-panic toward the direction of the Captain, sure by now that his inability to control the engine room telegraph was about to place *Iberia* in danger of collision, only to meet the fierce glower of the Captain himself, who held the starboard side telegraph handles firmly in his own hands.

'*Never* ring full astern on this ship, Cadet, unless at the express order of myself,' he growled, and with that he turned and strode after his ebullient bouncy Pilot, satisfied that his message had been well received, and all too aware of the scare he had left behind him.

Bridge Watch-Keeping duties were also required of Cadets as *Iberia* cruised between port calls, more so in the capacity of additional look-out or radar observer than anything else, except of course on the Watch held by her then Second Officer, who would later become P & O's Cadet Training Officer.

Despite the deteriorating eye-sight which he hotly denied, his passion was for cricket, and his Watch Cadet would have to look forward to much slip catching practice across the large expanse of Bridge deck during the afternoon watch, as the ship slipped quietly through the sparkling warm waters of the summer Mediterranean, heat haze sufficiently distant to allow early sighting of approaching shipping, between catches.

Only occasionally would ball sail from the Bridge to land among a sprawl of 1st Class passengers luxuriating in the hot sun on the deck above the children's nursery, just forward of the Bridge structure. The Second Officer would depart swiftly to the chartroom to allow the duty standby Quartermaster to gaze innocently down at the passengers' puzzled glances towards the Bridge.

His eventual arrival to Head Office as the Cadet Training Officer was marked by an upsurge in cricket fixtures between pre-sea training colleges, and the introduction of a Linguaphone course in Urdu as compulsory for all Cadets, reflective then of the almost total use of

Indian seamen throughout the P & O fleet. Each ship that carried
Cadets would be issued with a Dansette record player for exclusive
use of Cadet training in Urdu, and many a ship's party in Australia,
New Zealand, Colombo and so forth would subsequently bear
testimony to its misuse!

Of Quartermasters, here lay a strong vein of resentment against the
presence of Cadets on board during the cruising season, because it
would otherwise have fallen to them to cox the ship's boats at the
anchorage ports, to the obvious accumulation of much overtime
money now denied them. It would be overly cynical to believe that
P & O took this (not inconsiderable) saving to ledger when appoint-
ing Cadets for cruising, but undoubted saving it was.

'I've got more salt in me socks than you've bloody well sailed over,
son,' snarled one such Quartermaster, irritated beyond control by a
Cadet admonishing him for smoking whilst on the Bridge.

'In that case, you have apparently learned very little during the
experience,' came the icy response.

In the main, though, P & O Quartermasters in the passenger liners
(in the cargo ship fleet, the Quartermasters were Indian, their rating
'Secunny') were extremely competent, often having served with the
Royal Navy or Royal Marines before joining P & O. Some years
after *Iberia*, one of her then Cadets was serving as Second Officer in
Orcades, and of his two watch Quartermasters, one was nicknamed
'Black Jack', a name he had presumably gained during his time as a
Royal Marine.

Tall and strong, he stood attentively balanced behind the wheel as
Orcades drove through the 12–4 Watch night hours towards Bombay,
his lived-in face reflecting the green glow from the gyro compass
repeater before him, but at peace with the world.

Behind him, the Captain tiredly conducted one of India's
remaining Maharajahs through an impromptu bridge visit demanded
by his VIP passenger. Ignoring the wonders of the ship's photo-plot
radar the Maharajah placed his hand on the buttock of 'Black Jack'
and not realising how close he had placed himself to the killing edge
of unarmed combat, spoke the following immortal words:

'What a lovely bottom you have, my dear!' then allowed himself
to be led hurriedly away by the Officer of the Watch as *Orcades*

resumed her proper course, having been deflected therefrom by buttock clenching reaction from the enraged Quartermaster.

Barmen were a new breed of rating to Cadets fresh to liners, who, in giving scant recognition or attention to the itinerant presence of Cadets during cruising, probably failed to recognise the interest in their work that would be generated by this learning curve.

Ironic, therefore, was one of a series of advertisements that appeared in the national press during 1957, depicting the kindly face of a Verandah Café barman, the bar being in *Iberia*'s First Class accommodation, and much used by her cruising passengers.

The copy was a cocktail of superlatives, the message one of extreme comfort and went as follows:

'He is a student of sociability – yet a master of the art of creating it. He is a prince of pleasantness – yet subject to the whims and fancies of all who visit his domain. He is a magician with the skill and wherewithal to put a sharp edge on a dull appetite, or tune the raw edge off a deep depression, to quench a worthwhile thirst, or to light a glow that is "all glorious within". His cap is crowded with feathers from the famous cocktails he mixes. A birthday, any anniversary, or even just a jolly get-together for the fun of it – mention it to him, and for your enjoyment he will produce a touch of genius born of infinite care for others. He is the creator of cordial relations. He is the Verandah Café Barman on board the P & O ship *Iberia*. In helping to knit friendships between all who come under his benign influence, he is creating sound ties in the Commonwealth lifeline.'

He probably was outwardly a cheerful friendly chap, but to the Cadets now posted to the same ship, it came quickly to their notice, perhaps balanced as they were somewhere between Officers and Petty Officers, that appointment to the position of barman in any one of the ship's passenger bars was much sought after. Bar prices on board were ridiculously low to the average passenger, but even so they, the passengers, were blissfully unaware of the systematic 'milking' to which they were subjected, and the cynicism of those behind the bars that were depicted as 'princes of pleasantries, yet subject to the whims and fancies of all who visit their domains'. Passengers were there to be fleeced, and fleeced they were.

Some years later, one of *Iberia*'s Cadets for that 1957 cruising season was to travel home from Australia to the United Kingdom as a passenger in *Stratheden*, having spent some six months unpaid leave in Australia after serving as Third Officer in the *Aden*, the dreaded 'white crew' ship of the P & O cargo fleet.

Immediately made a member of the *Stratheden* Wardroom, he nevertheless luxuriated in the unique opportunity to make full use of all passenger facilities aboard, having personally paid the fare home. On departure from Sydney, his status within the P & O was nevertheless generally unknown, and this became very obvious as he took a sip from the ordered sun-downer. With a grimace of annoyance he recalled the steward who had served his drink and quietly brought to his attention that although a passenger, 'this particular user of your Bar is a serving P & O Officer who would much appreciate not being served from the watered down gin bottle again,' in sure knowledge that word would (as it did) quickly spread. The drink was replaced immediately, and whilst others suffered unwittingly the watered down versions as *Stratheden* completed her homeward voyage, he did not.

In common with all P & O Junior Officers, *Iberia*'s Cadets took their meals in the First Class restaurant, situated on 'D' deck, but were allocated two tables adjacent to the port side revolving door access to the kitchens, or galley more nautically described. White Mess Kit was mandatory dress for dinner in the Mediterranean.

Arrival to dinner was a rather breathless affair if the Cadets had been enjoying the Wardroom facilities just under the Bridge deck. The combination of fifteen minutes grace from the time of the dinner gong (later than that and you did not go to the restaurant), and the rule that Cadets were not allowed to use the passenger lifts saw frantic flight down the main staircase through some six decks. The final burst through the restaurant's revolving doors on 'D' deck, and the hurried walk the length of the restaurant to their tables was not infrequently greeted by a smatter of applause from some of the passengers.

On one unfortunate occasion, as *Iberia* lurched her way across the Bay of Biscay, such a phalanx of Cadets hit the revolving doors just as a middle-aged woman arrived thereto from the restaurant side, intent on swift departure to nurse the *mal-de-mer* that was so obviously about to give her public embarrassment.

Her look of incredulous amazement banished momentarily the vomitous grimace of only seconds before, as she whistled swiftly

MEDITERRANEAN CRUISING: *IBERIA* 117

through 180 degrees of exit, to spin, top-like, into 'D' deck lobby. She was followed by a quick-thinking Cadet who had completed a 360 degree turn through the doors in order to lend assistance where necessary. His thoughtfulness however went unnoticed, as the effect of such catapult action then combined with a ponderous roll of the ship, was to apply the *coup de grâce*! Happily, this was not a regular occurrence.

Surprisingly, during one cruise, two male passengers each in his mid to late fifties were seated at one of the Cadets' allotted tables, and it transpired that they had cruised regularly over the past years. Each evening they would arrive to the first sitting for dinner immaculate in white tuxedos, and invariably offer their young table companions wine – they were adamant on leaving that cruise in Southampton that they had never enjoyed themselves as much as they had in *Iberia* that year, and it must be said that if anyone got First Class treatment in the ship's launches, those gentlemen did.

Being adjacent to the kitchen access held its moments of high amusement too, as it was not unknown for collisions to occur as stewards carried emptied dishes back to the kitchens, and loaded dishes several orders high to their waiting passengers.

One such collision occurred between two stewards each of whom displayed a disproportionate number of female genes, and were therefore identified as 'queer'.

'Oh, you stupid bitch, look what you've done,' squealed one in falsetto tones clearly heard by many of *Iberia*'s diners.

'Your fault, you silly cow,' came in ringing response, and for moments thereafter a cacophonous theatre developed until the antagonists were separated by a harassed Restaurant Chief Steward, and peace restored to the restaurant.

One Goanese steward too, hands laden with plates, pushed the revolving door with his shoe, but with the unfortunate result that somehow his foot caught in one of the door components. His resulting one-foot hop through two revolutions of the doors carrying his heaped tray was worthy of vaudeville, and nimbly accomplished.

Knowledge of the devious workings of the kitchens' so-called 'dropsie' system also came to the amazed notice of Cadets, questioning as they were the slowness of service on the part of their Goanese steward, compared with the relative swiftness of others serving passenger tables.

Within the working structure of the galley were cold meat chefs, salad chefs, fish chefs, and more besides but spider-like at the centre of all this activity sat THE CHEF, his importance in the scheme of things unquestioned, his power in his sphere complete.

Simply defined, a steward would wish to impress his passengers by swift and competent service to maximise his opportunity for tips. To get appropriate attention from the many pantries or serving positions within the kitchens, and achieve the necessary speed of service, he would be required to 'drop' so much cash against anticipated tips to the variety of under-chefs, who in turn would be expected to 'drop' a sizable proportion to The Chef. The system was obviously self-defeating as far as passenger service went, but The Chef earned a handsome dividend in his little counting house in the galley. With tips from Cadets being rather sparse, their steward was unable to ride the system – that is, at least, until the Cadets found out, and introduced a little priority on their own behalf.

Activities of the galley were oft-times viewed askance from the Bridge, too, as the frenzy of activity that marked the washing up of myriad plates used during the serving of countless dishes reached an after-meal climax. Strolling on the Bridge wings, which in extremity overlooked the ship's side, the Officer of the Watch would perforce give glance astern, with a clear view of the vessel's length slipping through the irritation of foamed Mediterranean Sea that marked her passage. Not infrequently, hands clutching a pile of soiled plates would stretch forth from portholes opened from the galley, to drop them with marked splash into the sea. How many of P & O's platters were thuswise consigned to the watery deep is impossible to surmise, but suffice it to say that orders placed with suppliers to replace 'storm damaged' crockery were often inaccurate in their verbiage.

One of *Iberia*'s Cadets, serving some seven years later as Navigating Lieutenant, RNR in HMS *Repton*, a minesweeper of the Vernon Squadron, was to hear from the First Lieutenant that P & O was not alone in this rather expensive washing up procedure.

En route to America to demonstrate the then potential of the new breed of Britain's mine hunting vessels, the First Lieutenant's vessel had visited Bermuda, berthing on that part of the sparkling harbour normally occupied by the liner *Queen of Bermuda*, of the Furness Withy Company. Frogmen, diving to practise their skills, surfaced time after time to bring to their ship's sweep deck hundreds of top quality plates, many still stuck together by the original grease of eggs and bacon, cause of their casual dispatch to the bottom of Bermuda's harbour. It was said that the mess decks of that particular RN vessel were graced for some time after with their finds, the owners of the *Queen of Bermuda* having declined with some embarrassment to receive back their written-off stock.

Iberia's Cadets found that cruising was not all a whirl of social encounter, as many hours had to be spent in the preparing of boats for port calls where the vessel was unable to go alongside, and indeed many more in their actual running.

This function at times brought about a mind-numbing tiredness as they drove back and forth between ship and shore under the hot Mediterranean sun, and oft-times in the darkness that came so quickly, as passengers jostled and pushed for space aboard the 'Limos' or 'PBs' that came to bear them back to their waiting liner, so patiently and light-bedecked at anchor off shore.

Diplomacy and seamanship are a not unknown admixture of need, but both were often stretched to their limits by demands of passengers who so quickly learned to bay when confronted by perceived inconvenience, or weather that sometimes refused to conform to the brochures glossy. And what was the answer to the starry-eyed daughter who insisted on spending the whole day in the launch of her would-be beau aboard ship, mouthing, 'I love you,' to the continual embarrassment of the Cadet in charge, amid amused knowing glances of 'We've seen it all before' from itinerant cruisers.

Notwithstanding, there were moments of high value during the running of the boats, and no more so than at Palma that year, once *Iberia* had brought up to anchor, preparatory to sending her invasion force of boated passengers through the harbour to shore-side amusement.

It was customary to nominate a 'path finder' launch at boating ports, the task of the Cadet coxswain being to lead the other boats over the safest and most direct path to whatever landing point was nominated by local Agents. To this end, the appropriate chart was carefully perused prior to the first boat departure from the ship's side.

That particular bright warm morning, a 'Limousine' was the first to speed shorewards, her tourist class complement of passengers brightly and excitedly reflecting the day's atmosphere. The Cadet in charge worriedly consulted the folded chart on his minuscule Bridge, aware of his responsibility to those boats that one by one fell into his wake, themselves heavily laden with P & O's life-blood.

Satisfied that all was well, his sun-glassed eyes were suddenly drawn to a large black-hulled yacht that lay alongside ahead and to port, instantly recognisable as *Scirroco*, the yacht of Errol Flynn. Curious, and forgetting his path-finder status momentarily, he eased his 'Limo' to port, in order to pass close to this famous craft, and obediently his followers altered in turn to trace his track. Equally curious, those of his passengers in open deck seating followed the direction of the Cadet's gaze, and as word quickly spread, so excited attention was bestowed upon the soon-to-be unhappy owner of this most famous of yachts.

Errol sat in the sternsheets of his craft, and without costume and make-up, looked distinctly old and world-weary as he sipped his breakfast orange juice.

'Yoo-hoo, Errol!' sounded out as the Cadet brought his launch past the yacht, the cry being taken up by all aboard, and as each successive launch rocked him in its passing, so his quiet *petit déjeuner* reverberated to a rising and unwanted public cacophony of early morning British public adoration.

Whilst it is doubtful that all 1,300 passengers screamed 'Yoo-hoo, Errol,' suffice it to say that sufficient did to persuade him to put to sea with some haste, only to face the raucous calls of *Iberia*'s off-duty European stewards' complement as he passed the ship at anchor, en route for quieter waters.

'Oy, Errol, what price bloody Burma now!' and other questioning greetings, too Anglo-Saxon and suggestive to repeat. His baleful glare in response said it all, and equalled any screen success of the silent movie era.

It was in such 'boat ports' that the then difference between First and Tourist Class would most manifest itself, as at sea the two parts of the ship were clearly segregated ('First Class passengers only beyond this point', read as 'Tourist Class passengers only past this point' on the reverse), and never the twain were supposed to twixt. A reasonable attitude in consideration of the prices paid for a cruise, and the fact that the marketing men had yet to come to the point where all would have equal access to the ship's facilities, albeit that cabin accommodation would vary in both location and comfort according to price paid.

The general effect was to ensure that, undoubtedly as a function of price, First Class passengers were usually older and more staid, whereas the Tourist end of the ship saw a zestier and more vibrant group approach to the cruise. That it was a launch from the Tourist gangway that path-found past Errol's yacht probably explained the festive attitude to his 'discovery', but it certainly caught on.

Return to the ship by launch was always a 'one class' ride, however, as it was impossible to allocate or schedule to separate gangways, Tourist or First Class. It was on these occasions that Tourist Class passengers, having rejoined the ship over the First Class gangway, would wander wide-eyed through First Class public rooms, hopefully encouraged to travel First Class next time around.

Strangely, Cadets were discouraged from socialising in the Tourist Class public rooms, whereas they were so encouraged toward attending dances and so forth in the First Class section of the ship (albeit with strong admonishment to be 'off decks' by 10.30 p.m., and 10 p.m. for Middle Watch keepers), probably on the premise that left to their own devices, they would probably gravitate towards the more boisterous Tourist group, and enjoy themselves far too late into the night.

Extracts from P & O Regulations, reprint dated 31 October 1956

Discipline.

Mixing with passengers.
'Joining in with the social life of passengers and sharing their amusements is attractive to some Officers, and not to others. It may add to the efficient running of the ship, and it may detract from it. It offers certain risks. It is a privilege and it carries a direct responsibility.'
 . . . 'It is not desirable for Women Officers to use the Verandah Café or Smoking Room.'
 . . . 'No Officer is to entertain a lady by herself in his cabin.'
 . . . 'The freedom with which various Officers are entrusted is a recognition that they are responsible persons who can be trusted to

behave as such. But they must realise that it holds out certain dangers to their career which would be avoided if they were not to mix socially with passengers. Inability to do themselves credit in public will mean inability to remain in the Company, for service in the Company requires the ability of an Officer to mix socially with passengers and yet to stand up to any problems which this may involve.

.... 'The wife of an Officer shall not travel as passenger in any ship in which the Officer is serving, except where expressly permitted to do so.'

Deck Officers, exalted positions toward which Cadets aspired, were encouraged to mix socially during off-duty hours, but were positively discouraged from entertaining passengers of the opposite sex in their cabins beneath the Bridge deck, which brought about as a direct result the time-honoured game of 'wheeling in' to achieve just that, essential prerequisite to possible light hearted seduction.

In this, the geography of *Iberia*, and indeed her sister *Arcadia*, lent itself more readily to the anonymous escorting of First Class passengers to the dizzy heights, rather than Tourist Class, as the latter would entail a somewhat hazardous public traverse of the ship's length, either along open decks or through accommodation alley-ways, prior to reaching the relative safety of the service pantries that connected vertically up through the First Class decks to the Navigating Officers' accommodation.

Engineers and Purser Officers suffered no such class disadvantage, with their cabins being situated on decks that afforded almost direct access to both First and Tourist public spaces. Cadets too, with passenger cabins on 'D' deck as their allocated quarters, were theoretically better placed for such 'wheeling in' activities than their qualified Seniors, a situation not necessarily to the liking of the Chief Officer in his rate of surrogate headmaster. Not, of course, that Cadets highly motivated in the work ethic chose to involve themselves in such games, particularly constrained as they were by being berthed two to a cabin!

'Listen, bloke, would you mind wandering about the decks for a few hours this evening? There's this particularly attractive girl from Liss that's interested in chess, and three really is a crowd.'

'Well, as a matter of fact, I was going to mention to you that there's a girl from Dumbarton interested in opera, and we were planning to play a few records together on your player this evening, if you can find somewhere to go for a while.'

Impasse, saved only by the ship's system of 'dropsie', this time applicable to temporary acquisition of a spare cabin on 'A' deck, achieved by 'dropping' a pound or two of currency to the 'A' deck cabin steward, who by chance was friendly with Biff Kemp, Steward *extraordinaire* to his young gentlemen.

None of this had been taught at *Conway*, *Worcester*, Pangbourne or Warsash, nor indeed as mountains and lakes were overcome variously at Outward Bound schools – notwithstanding '*Quis Nos Separabit*', motto of the P & O, now had a relevance! For anyone who has not so set tryst, the agony of transporting illicit and costly (to a Cadet) gin – 'Christ, bloke, I don't know what she'll drink, and I can't afford whisky' – from 'D' to 'A' deck with 1,300 passengers now watching, let alone the Captain and his entire complement of officers, it is heart pumpingly different, and the thought of discovery within the relative opulence of said 'A' deck cabin definitely no aphrodisiac, as undoubtedly testified to by the occasional equally apprehensive, but eventually unsullied, maidens.

Some few years later, one of *Iberia*'s Cadets, now a Junior Officer on *Arcadia* en route for Australia, was to find himself yet again in an 'A' deck cabin, sent thereto by his Senior Officer on the Bridge to investigate persistent complaints from the female occupant of 'unceasing noise of a typewriter'.

It was during a stormy 12–4 watch, with the ship lurching its way through heavy seas, temperature even on the Bridge demanding greatcoats and gloves to keep out the cold, and the clear-glass screens in the Bridge front windows whirling through their hurried circles to hurl rain and sea spume away.

Thus clad, be-capped and with binoculars still slung round his neck on a shortened strap, the Third Officer met with the Night Watchman and knocked on the cabin door. Bidden to enter he did so, and before the Night Watchman could follow him, *Arcadia* rolled heavily to starboard, and the cabin door slammed shut. The occupant, female, Caucasian and with obvious nymphomaniac tendencies wrapped her arms of some forty summers round the startled young officer's neck, and ignoring the drips of rainwater from the peak of his uniform cap that fell onto her nightgown, made an immediate and suggestive invitation as to how they should spend the immediate next moments, and indeed others en route to Australia.

With difficulty he extricated himself from her embrace, and with binoculars rattling against greatcoat buttons, wrenched open the cabin door and made an undignified withdrawal to the alleyway, assuring Madame that her complaint would be investigated by the Bureau come dawn, and delivering a furious reprimand to the white-jacketed nightwatchman for his failure to add physical support during the past awful moments. With his otherwise boring night of tedious making of tea and toast thus relieved by the Officer's discomfort, the nightwatchman chuckled his way back to his night pantry, whilst the Third Officer beat a hasty retreat back to the Bridge. Suffice it to say that no more typewriter noises were reported for the remainder of the voyage to Sydney, where the occupant of that particular cabin disembarked.

Off-duty Cadets were expected to attend Gala Night and Fancy Dress dances, with the strict understanding that each was to apportion equal time to dancing with different age groups rather than give obvious and disproportionate attention to unattached daughters of their own age. The Fancy Dress nights were of less interest as the inevitable 'Suzy Gone Wong' or 'Day and Night' would be led, cruise after cruise, into the 'parade ring' by the Quartermaster or Entertainments Officer, but Gala Nights were usually inspiring, and vastly surpassed any of the mundane social events arranged aboard the cargo ships, even in port.

The Gala atmosphere would pervade even for dinner, as garlands and streamers festooned the dining room and each place seating was allocated a funny hat, even those of the Cadets. Wine would flow with greater ease than normal, and aware of Cadets' usual state of poverty, passengers quite often would bestow some bottles of Bacchus cheer as gifts to the young gentlemen who were always suitably grateful, and sometimes somewhat frolicsome thereafter as a direct consequence. On one such night, with the midnight witching hour fast approaching, and the likelihood of the Chief Officer choosing to check that his charges were safely tucked up, Cadet Peter was noted as missing. Missing, that is, in the sense that he had failed to verify his whereabouts to his fellow Cadets, such that appropriate cover could be given in the event of need.

'Cadet Peter, sir? He's in one of our cabins, sir, and we'll have him call you back straight away.' The fact that Cadet Peter would then call from an 'A' deck cabin, Engineer Officer's cabin, Woman Assistant Purser's cabin or whatever, was undetectable in the call back, always provided that background noise was properly controlled.

Cadet Peter was, however, missing, AWOL, out of central control and therefore probably in need of assistance. Search was commenced as surreptitiously as possible through passenger public rooms, and Peter was eventually found wandering happily along the brightly lit port promenade deck, fortunately and unusually devoid of passengers, singing quietly to himself repeated verses of 'A Wild Colonial Boy' in his distinctly Irish brogue, with bow tie untied, and the ends by no means hiding the patch of spilled Martini that blushed his white mess jacket.

Placing his forefinger across his pursed lips he hissed a solemn 'Shuuush' to his discoverers as they urged him towards the pantry 'bolt hole' that would give undetected descent to the safety of 'D' deck, 'you'll wake the bloody passengers,' and laughed uproariously at his own perception.

To 'D' deck he was eventually urged and so to rest, but only after he had spent some few minutes solemnly polishing the floor of 'D' deck foyer with an electric polishing machine left unattended by one of the night cleaners – it must have been a time of mental throw-back to his training ship days, and an overpowering compulsion once again to polish decks. A person of powerful build and emotions, he was to have his mother in tears one day between cruises in Southampton, confirming to her horrified ears that so much time had elapsed since his last attendance to confession that he felt himself unable to unburden himself in the priesthood's limited time.

His must have been a perceived burden, because cruising Cadets were kept far too busy to be anything else but innocents abroad.

In later cruising years, P & O, as others, would introduce a wide range of entertainment for passengers provided by professional entertainers, bridge players, golf instructors and many others. *Iberia*, however, then had to be mainly content with the ship's band, fancy dress nights, and racing nights with deck tennis, deck quoits, and cricket during the daylight hours. All this was painstakingly organised and controlled by the Staff Captain and his small team composed of

Entertainment Officer, two Entertainment Hostesses and Quarter-masters, the last seconded from normal Bridge duties.

That season, however, three Cadets, after initial and critical exposure to the Officers' Wardroom, were called upon to lend their occasional amateur presence to Gala Night festivities, having practised and formed themselves into a skiffle group, skiffle being the rage of the time.

Under the artistic guidance of Cadet Keith on guitar, and with Cadets Harry and John providing support on tea-chest bass and washboard respectively, the Iberians (for so they were called, and what else?) provided endless hours of rapturous and closely har-monised entertainment to enthralled passengers. The truth of that retrospective statement may be slightly distorted by time, but the Iberians took great pleasure from their newly acquired art form, and were later to flourish again as they came together in yet another P & O liner – more of that later, however.

Practice had perforce to be done in the baggage rooms, and, astonishingly, in their own time, the Chief Officer stubbornly refusing to allow such artistic innovation to take precedence over the need to service and clean the passenger launches. His shortsightedness would doubtless have been shared by the then Board of Trade Examiners of Masters and Mates, being uninterested in the breaking strain of a Ceylon tea-chest bass string (about two gin and tonics and an Allsopps beer) and the stowage factor of ten sewing thimbles, which equated to roughly one pocket of the S.W. Silver & Company standard white mess-jacket. Neither would the washboard have interested him, other perhaps than in a moment of unguarded nostalgia, something for which Examiners of Masters and Mates were not particularly renowned.

Correct uniform dress code at all times was insisted upon by P & O although during the night watch it was sometimes accepted that the Officers of the Watch could relax this code somewhat, although that was by no means general throughout the passenger ship fleet, and depended very much upon the Captain. Some indeed would insist that not only would the OOW take over his Watch in the correct rig of the day (or night) but further would wear his uniform cap throughout the Watch. Unexpected visits to the Bridge by some Captains would be effected not as a check on ship's position or safety, but on the dress of those on duty thereon, which brought about situations that would later bring forth laughter in the recounting, but some trepidation at the time.

As the Junior Officer of the Watch in *Oriana* some few years on, one of *Iberia*'s Cadets experienced just one of those occasions, as the Captain appeared on the Bridge at 2 a.m. to sign his Night Orders, still immaculately dressed in tropical mess-kit and formidably pompous as ever. The Junior Officer, bare-headed as he placed the ship's 'fix' on the chart, was wearing open necked uniform shirt with epaulettes of rank, white tropical shorts, long white cotton socks and white buckskin shoes, this rig having been deemed perfectly acceptable for the night's 'dead watch' in his previous appointment, another large liner of the P & O fleet.

He glanced up from the pool of harsh white light that illuminated the chart table as the Captain spoke and then stood respectfully erect in recognition of the presence.

'Tell the Senior Officer of the Watch to report to me,' the Captain hummed, and the Third Officer ducked quickly through the thick black curtain that kept light away from the darkened wheelhouse, to so pass the Captain's summons.

'The Old Man wants you, sir,' and the First Officer, hastily ramming on his uniform cap, passed through into the chartroom.

He reappeared some moments later. 'The Captain wants to see you, bloke, and don't forget your cap.'

'But he's just seen me,' hissed the Third Officer quietly, reaching to retrieve his cap perched atop the radar screen.

'Yes, but you weren't wearing your cap,' the First Officer grinned quietly back, and bade his 'winger' return to the chartroom with jerk of his thumb.

With head now suitably covered to satisfy the catholicism of the moment, the Third Officer slipped back into the light of the chartroom, and the waiting Captain who stood, with hands behind his back, eyes fixed on the chart before him.

'What sort of rig do you call that, boy?' questioned the Master, not deigning to look at the young officer.

'Night steaming rig, sir,' was the response, and the Orient Line Captain sighed in exasperation as he glanced in pained enquiry at the P & O officer at his side.

'And what was your last vessel?' came the next question, doubtless anticipating the name of one of the P & O cargo ships as explanation for the displayed heresy of not dressing in white No. 10s.

'*Canberra*, sir,' came the proud reply, albeit surprised at the apparent blind spot in the Captain's memory.

'And before that?' probed the Captain.

'*Maloya*, sir,' and the Captain, satisfied now that he had made his point, signed his Night Orders, and made ponderous departure from the Bridge to his bed. *Maloya* was one of P & O's first ventures into tankers!

So it was that *Iberia*'s Cadets paid punctilious attention to their code of uniform dress, ably assisted by the ship's laundry that would deliver back shirts and collars, long white uniform trousers and jackets so heavily starched as to make entry into these items of clothing an art in itself. This was particularly so during the rush that usually accompanied the task as working gear was hurriedly discarded and a pre-lunch pour-out slotted into the fifteen minutes grace pattern.

Panting but triumphant, and foregathered with Pinocchio stiffness into one of the four cabins on 'D' deck, the morning's triumphs or failures would be briefly discussed, laughter would pervade the cabin's narrow confines, and the bright Mediterranean sunshine would spill through the single porthole, through the haze of cigarette smoke and onto the gleaming fresh 'whites' of the freshly scrubbed gathering.

Cadet Simon, as host at one such pre-lunch pour-out, officiated at the opening of the Allsopps cans of beer, although he himself had a penchant for Guinness. It was indeed a can of Guinness that he attacked somewhat imprudently with the sharp-pointed opener, failing to apply the mandatory two sharp taps on the can that Biff Kemp, steward *extraordinaire*, had instructed as a means to tame the gaseous content prior to opening. Ireland's best, summoned thus, leapt forth from the can in Simon's left hand and he, mindful of the black-haired wrath that could spring from the Cadet immediately before him, squealed a loud and lisped warning to that son of Dublin as he thereupon swung the can swiftly to his left.

'Look out, Peetah,' he beseeched, as the black liquid contents hissed and splashed merrily onto the pristine virginal starch of the uniform next to him, and 'Peetah' collapsed into roars of Irish laughter at the distress and discomfiture of the luckless recipient.

'S-sorry, bloke,' scarcely sufficed, and *Iberia*'s first-sitting passengers, as they streamed into the First Class restaurant, had perforce to sympathise with the unfortunate Cadet as he made his unhappy way across 'D' deck foyer to his own cabin on the starboard side of the ship, his S.W. Silver & Company's finest be-spattered from collar to crotch in this by-product of the famed Liffey river.

As his fellow Cadets guffawed and spilled their way into the restaurant for their Penang curry or whatever, the upset was slightly mollified by the thoughtful arrival of Biff Kemp, steward *extraordinaire*, armed with plate of steak rolls, his Masonic seniority as always overriding the galley system of 'dropsie'.

'For one of my young gentlemen, Chef, what's been inconvenienced,' and Fagan of the kitchen would smile understandingly.

Not surprisingly, and in common with many of those that spent their lives shifting from one combination of uniform to another, dress sense in terms of colour combinations when proceeding on leave was rarely a strength, and cause oft-times of stifled laughter, or even open derision from those who had to suffer in company with the metamorphosis.

'If you think that I'm going to be seen on the beach at Estoril with you in that gear you've another think coming!' How narrow-minded were the young ladies of the mid-fifties. Green shorts, grey open-necked shirt, knee-length white uniform socks and brown suede chukka boots seemed most appropriate after the inevitable uniform, especially for a beach outing, so a sad set-down that preceded shame-faced change.

For three Cadets of *Iberia* that year in Venice, however, no such concern as they sallied forth to enjoy the night life of that famed city, wearing as they did the borrowed finery of their collective group of eight, with the good wishes of the five remaining on board, ringing in their ears.

They strolled nonchalantly down the First Class gangway, undetectable from the richest aboard in their white tuxedos, dress shirts and black bow ties, black dress trousers and gleaming black dress shoes, with only the grin and knowing wink from the duty Quartermaster to mark their passing, his salute, whilst unexpected, saying 'good on you, lads.'

A casual stroll along the water's edge towards St Mark's Square in the evening's summer balm preceded their arrival to the nightclub of their choice, and having been ushered to a table, one immediately invited a young lady, strangely unescorted, to dance, leaving his companions to order whatever refreshments caught their fancy. His flushed return some bars of music later, anticipating something different from Allsopps, was greeted by rigid inactivity.

'Look at the bloody pricelist,' hissed one of his companions, and so bid, he did.

Moments later, and with as much dignity as they could muster, the three made their way to the door and to financial sanity, only temporarily embarrassed by the manager of the premises who said quite loudly, 'Good night, gentlemen, and thank you very much for the dance.' His English was unfortunately perfect.

The evening hours were thus whiled away in St Mark's Square with an extraordinarily inexpensive bottle of wine, as orchestras various enchanted the tourists. That experience was surpassed en route back to the ship by an unexpected happening by two off-duty gondoliers. They, completely oblivious to on-lookers and lounging comfortably in their moored gondola beneath a bridgespan, played mandolin and guitar in a perfect expression of seeming contentment, no doubt partially induced by the day's takings from *Iberia*'s passengers.

Venice on that cruise was marked in more sombre, albeit majestic, manner, brought about by the death of one of the Goanese stewards and the subsequent funeral departure from the ship.

From *Iberia*'s white hull there swept away a long, black gondola, propelled therefrom by some six black-clad gondoliers, the coffin, itself black, on the narrow deck between them. It seemed somehow a most fitting exit for that son of Goa, his country converted to Catholicism by the Portuguese; his passing afforded the full pomp of his gained faith, not so very far from Rome. How much more appropriate than the stilted service for burial at sea, and the impersonal stitching of rough canvas shroud that was more often the way.

Cannes was another cruise port that saw *Iberia*'s Cadets ashore in the evening, although lessons learned in Venice as to the nightclub scene saw them casually dressed and really anticipating nothing more than a quiet stroll among the rich, and perhaps a glass or two of French beer. It was therefore somewhat of a surprise to find themselves in what appeared to be a nightclub, and able to afford the price of the house beer.

This magnificently appointed spot was named 'Les Trois Cloches', and appeared quite sumptuous in its red brocade decor, and cheerfully friendly as young waitresses weaved their busy way between the tables, directed by an older woman of ample proportions, heavily made up, her many chins wobbling with good humour. There was a floorshow too, with nubile young ladies frolicking through their dance routines before an appreciative audience, swelled tonight by five of *Iberia's* nine Cadets.

Cadet Simon was well pleased with himself as quite obviously he had somehow caught the attention of the amply proportioned *chef de salon*, to the point where she would, on passing the table, lean over and give his cheek an affectionate pinch, the while winking quite outrageously at him. Such attention and interest must surely bring with it, at the very least, a free glass of something.

It did of course, and Simon chortled his glee, then blissfully unaware of being the butt of some particular joke. Indeed he was the last to realise that which was becoming increasingly apparent to his fellow Cadets. Every female member of the staff, and indeed the nubile young ladies of the floorshow – all were male! Even Simon's ample benefactor, now seen as grotesque in rouge and lipstick (at least to Simon) was at least born to the male gender although little remained visibly apparent now.

Surrounded by his discomfort and by stalwart chums who found the whole scene uproariously funny, huffy but haughty departure was made from the Three Bells at Cannes, and yet another experience clocked up to stand them all in good stead for the future.

'Christ, blokes, you could have told a chap,' he scolded, and then joined the laughter that followed.

Another attraction offered to passengers was the opportunity to visit the ship's Navigating Bridge, and this was eagerly taken up by most. For the Cadets, these visits represented another duty to be performed, assisting in the ushering of visiting groups through the Bridge tours, and answering such questions as came their way from people eager to learn the secrets of navigation, the theory of radar and such as radio direction-finding.

It was of course a full uniform occasion, and not at all unimpressive therefore for the passengers. Usually, and to ensure that the Officer of the Watch had uninterrupted overview of the ship's approach through the water, an area forward of the steering position was roped off and he, the OOW, would stand within this holy ground, binoculars slung casually round his neck for image.

The Second Officer of the *Iberia*, however, always went one better, for he would pace his allotted space with the ship's large brass telescope carried beneath his arm, and no-one would know that its use was infrequent, if ever! The occasional golf stroke practice with the telescope, or a late cut through the covers similarly enacted, only served to heighten the allusion that the officer was not only widely travelled, but rather a play-boy to boot.

Often, if no other shipping was within clear horizon distance, the OOW would give brief but succinct explanation of the gyro and magnetic compasses that were positioned before the Quartermaster, and the Cadet stationed on the so called 'Monkey Island' deck above the wheelhouse, would demonstrate the checking of compass alignment via the speaking tube.

'What are the two round iron objects on the side of the magnetic compass?' would be the question most eagerly anticipated, and the response would be solemnly intoned with practised delivery, having first ensured no clerics were present.

'Lord Kelvin brought this particular magnetic compass into commercial application, and as with all magnetic compasses, quadrantal deviation has to be corrected with soft iron spheres. For this particular compass, therefore, they are referred to as Lord Kelvin's balls.'

In actual fact, the need to be knowledgeable as to the various navigational instruments and their uses came as a useful addition to the Cadets' studies, as to be unprepared for an indepth discussion with an interested passenger was at very least an embarrassment, if not a bad reflection upon the Company. At worst, word would undoubtedly get back to the Commander.

Some years later, in *Oriana*, an American male of some fifty-five summers caused such frustration at the Ship's Office (Bureau) in his demand for a private (not with other passengers) visit to the Bridge that to keep peace in the valley, the First Officer agreed to accept such a visit during his afternoon 12-4 watch, and so it came about. He and his Third Officer 'winger' gave their full attention to their lone visitor, save for the need to keep a wary eye out for other shipping, and were at great pains to ensure that every question was met with reasoned response and appropriate explanation.

His visit finally and thankfully at an end, the demanding American turned to the First Officer, a pleasant and unflappable person known rarely to display anger or even irritation, save perhaps in a slight stutter that would sometimes develop in times of stress.

'Well, you fellas appear to know something about what you're doing,' he pontificated, 'and it makes me proud as an American to know that Vasco de Gama, who was an American, invented navigation.'

With that, he demanded to be led below by the Third Officer, leaving an incredulous First Officer in the centre of the wheelhouse as *Oriana* sped her way across the Pacific. The passenger failed to see the Senior Officer push his uniform cap to the back of his head, but could scarcely have failed to hear his exasperated and out of character explosion:

'Well, I-I'll be b-buggered!'

Other visits to the Bridge were sometimes much greater cause for alarm, as one of *Iberia*'s Cadets was to learn when serving as Second Officer in *Orsova* some years later.

At 2 a.m., half way through the midnight to 4 a.m. 'death watch', as the ship pushed through a plankton-sprinkled Indian Ocean, a Scottish lass materialised on the starboard Bridge wing clad only in dripping swimsuit, persuaded thereto from the party around the swimming pool by an obviously injudicious excess of alcohol. With the Captain due any minute to check all was well, before retiring, it was a much relieved Officer of the Watch who managed to persuade this threat to his career to vacate the Bridge, and for the next hour and a half he congratulated himself on his diplomacy, the Captain having appeared only seconds after the visitor's damp and giggling departure.

At 4.30 a.m., having handed over the Watch to his relieving Officer and completed the log book entries, he descended from the Bridge to a well-earned rest in his cabin two decks below, only to find Goldilocks, still attired in her wet costume, asleep in his bed! The subsequent awaking and removal of the damp, dishevelled and by now obviously hung-over late reveller through passenger accommodation, thankfully free of passengers, was accomplished with much

trauma and lack of diplomacy, and the eventual return to a wet bed
with distaste. Sighted some hours later by the Second Officer as he
took a turn round the decks before noon 'sights', she was blankly
unaware of her nocturnal escapades, choosing to sunglass her eyes
from the sun's glare reflecting from his white uniform.

The Bridge, of course, was the nerve centre of the ship, as well as
the centre of most pomp and ceremony, and it was from its august
height that the 'day's run' was solemnly announced by the Officer of
the Watch over the public address system, once the ship's Officers
had 'fixed' the vessel's noonday position, ably assisted during the
cruising season by Cadets in training.

Deck tennis would temporarily halt, books would be put down,
and conversation buzz generally hush as, firstly, the reaching of noon
was signalled by the formal striking of eight bells on the ship's bell,
followed by the disciplined and well modulated tones of the Officer
of the Watch.

'This is the Officer of the Watch speaking. Since our departure
from Tenerife, *Iberia* has steamed a distance of 270 nautical miles, at
an average speed of 17.26 knots.'

He would then continue by highlighting landmarks of interest and
times of intended passing, as well as brief observations on anticipated
weather conditions. Such moments were waited upon and repeated
daily in P & O liners across the world, and it would be true to say
that these noonday announcements achieved a great degree of
reverent and rapt attention.

What this attentive and over-awed audience was not able to see,
however, was the degree of self-control so often needed by the officer
making the announcement. Once he had commenced to speak, his
position was constrained by the knowledge that not only were all
passenger ears attentive, but also those of the ship's Commander, ever
critical in listening for fault from his Bridge. For the uninitiated
Cadets, therefore, it was with open-mouthed astonishment that they
would sometimes observe other officers solemnly allow the uniform
trousers of the Officer of the Watch to fall around his ankles as he
intoned his message, or immobilise his movement by tying the laces
of each shoe together.

So the cruising season continued, with Southampton as turn-
around port between each cruise. These were the opportunities for

P & O Cadets to see liners of other companies that plied routes different to these of P & O, such as Cunard's '*Queens*', Union Castle's '*Castle*' ships, and those of Safmarine, the South African flag carrier, to name but a few. There was the introduction to and adoption of the Red Lion by Bargate, and brief fleeting visits from fond parents, all agog to see the current palatial circumstances of their offspring and to take home glowing reports and not a few photographs.

Ports of call came and went with now practised familiarity, and Palma, Cannes, Madeira, Vigo, Izmir, Athens, Las Palmas, Kos, Gibraltar, Lisbon, Naples all slipped past into a blasé blur.

'The black hulled ship, now passing on our port side, is the P & O cargo ship *Sunda*, homeward bound from the Far East.'

There was a feeling of some superiority to sight fellow Cadets less grandly employed, fed, and entertained as they in turn glued envious binoculared eyes to watch *Iberia*'s high white profile sweep past, and leapt to dip ensign to the senior ship that bellowed her vast fog-horns in gracious greeting across the narrow stretch of water that divided the two vessels.

Young fingers that only a few short weeks ago fumbled, now nimbled the black bow tie of evening mess-kit into practised shape, and the young gentlemen were very much a part of the ship in their acquired knowledge and gathered expertise in handling their launches. That the cruising season was shortly to come to an end was regrettable in many ways, but much more work had to be done in other spheres prior to the sitting of professional examinations, and so thoughts of return to P & O's cargo fleet came not fully amiss, and in fact was largely welcome after three months total exposure to Britain's cruising public.

So it was that on Sunday 1 September 1957, the Commander of *Iberia*, together with his Senior Officers, joined the ship's Junior Officers that were off-duty in the wardroom, brought together by a simple invitation from the nine Cadets that cruised in her that season, as a token of appreciation not only for their acceptance on board, but also in respect for the standards and quality that prevailed in the ship. P & O had every reason to be proud. The green edged card read simply:

> ### P & O S.S. *IBERIA*
>
> The Cadets of the *Iberia* request the pleasure
> of the company of
>
> _____
>
> to a Cocktail Party in the Wardroom
> on Sunday, 1st September at 6.15pm
>
> Carriages at 7.15pm				Dress formal

It was the way, and three months and sixteen days after first sighting *Iberia* in London's Royal Docks, the nine took their trunks, together with assorted acquired castanets and other souvenir bric-a-brac, down the long wooden gangway that once again stretched from King George V dockside to *Iberia*'s 'D' deck tourist class access area. For each there would be a period of home leave that would probably stretch to ten days, and thereafter a further appointment back to the workhorses of the fleet, the cargo ships, dependant upon the whim of the personnel department

Merchant Navy Defence Course

For some Cadets however, and in absence of an immediate sea-appointment after leave, there was inclusion in a Merchant Navy Defence Course for a brief ten days. This involved total attention to the tender words and worldly reflections of the Chief Petty Officer RN resident in HMS *Chrysanthenum*, alongside the London Embankment.

As a Midshipman RNR the course held particular interest, although the art of loading and firing a 4 inch gun seemed to have little relevance to advances in Naval warfare by then achieved. As chance would have it, the Royal Naval Reserve 'P' course attendance some two years on as a Sub-Lieutenant RNR saw a reintroduction to the self-same equipment, so perhaps Naval statisticians had indeed not seen further than the 4 inch gun for Merchant Naval defence, after all.

So it was, therefore, that unknown to the general public that strolled the Embankment during those few days, deep in the bowels of the pretty little 'Flower' Class corvette, something stirred as Chief Petty Officer (G) brought to the ken of his avidly attentive group the mysteries of Naval warfare, or defence more correctly stated.

How best to insert the shell into the breech without total loss of fingers as the breech mechanism slammed shut was emphasised by the somewhat startling revelation that to do it his way as instructed was safe 'as long as human arses point downwards', a not insignificant span of reassurance that commanded the total obedience of his group.

'You try and tickle this lady the wrong way, gentlemen, and you won't come back for more.'

His words were to have a strong relevance two years on as a fellow P & O Officer, also Royal Naval Reserve, attempted to load a 4 inch shell (armed) into the waiting breech of a left gun at full elevation. Twice or even three times it slid backwards from the breech toward the concrete gun platform, to the fascinated and paralysed gaze of his fellow gun-crew members who, whilst perhaps sympathetic to his distress, were totally unwilling to see the human posterior assume anything but its normal downward direction, however momentarily. Fortunately training and a string of horrendous invective from the Petty Officer in charge of the gun achieved the necessary, the connectors snapped shut, and the shell lofted away on its mission of defence.

However, all good things were to come to an end, and with a cruising season now augmented by a total knowledge as to how best to defend one's ship, all that remained was for further sea-going appointments to be notified. It was back to reality!

CHAPTER 13

The Australian Run: *Pinjarra/Strathaird*

B UILT IN 1944 AND NAMED *Empire Paragon*, the vessel was orginally
owned by the Ministry of War and managed by the Ellerman
Wilson Line. It was in 1946 that she was renamed *Pinjarra*, although
presumably her original classifiaction as 'standard fast cargo liner',
remained unchanged, and as given to her by the builders, Sir James
Laing of Sunderland. Her 500 ft length compared to 64 ft beam gave
her alarming whip in any sort of a seaway, disconcerting to the
inexperienced, but her most endearing feature was that the disposition of the funnel to the square accommodation block ensured that
an almost continuous supply of smoke, soot and fumes were drawn
into the after accommodation doors and port-holes (no windows
here), for liberal dispersal throughout the cabins.

The Cadets' accommodation was carefully planned to the extreme
after end of the accommodation block and her complement of four
Cadets spent much time in cleaning their four-berth cabin and
attached study, whilst imitating the black and white minstrels. She
was a rugged cargo ship without pretension, her only concession
being a canvas constructed swimming pool that would be erected,
between ports, on the foredeck, but with space for little else. It was
back, too, to the carriage of racehorses, and an ostler role for the
Cadets, for which a small financial benefit would accrue from the
Chief Officer.

Ironically and while the P & O had been compared in literature to
the 'Coldstream Guards of the Merchant Navy', there did exist no
small degree of experience within Cadet ranks in the case of such
equestrian cargo, although questions pertaining to the care of horses
were noticeably missing from the curriculum for Masters and Mates,
surely an oversight of opportunity.

Pinjarra was essentially a happy ship, then engaged on the
Australian trade route. Her Captain was an endearingly bluff rough
diamond who seemed to stand little chance of commanding one of
the large white liners, but who seemed to care little for that. His

138

competence was unquestioned, but somehow he did not seem to fit the role demanded in the liners, one of almost constantly being accessible to passengers.

The Chief Officer by comparison was destined for passenger ships, and save for the rather unfortunate habit of whistling to gain the attention of his Cadets, demonstrated a smoothness that was to ensure the soon-to-be transition. Actually, his whistle approach did come to an abrupt halt when one Cadet, irritated beyond caring by the whistle, the heat that prevailed at the time in the Indian Ocean, and the ever-present soot factor snapped.

'For Christ's sake, sir, stop whistling at me. I'm not your bloody dog.'

Alarmed by his own outburst, but defiant to the end, his chin went up aggressively as was his wont in moments of stress, only to drop in surprise at the crisply delivered apology from the Chief Officer. Notwithstanding the apology, the Cadet was to lead a dog's life for some days thereafter!

Notwithstanding her cargo ship role, *Pinjarra* was nevertheless P & O, and despite her sooty environment, was to be seen as one in her adherence to flag etiquette, and not least of all, to her Officers and Cadets conforming to P & O's uniform regulations. Once into the Mediterranean and en route for Australia, blue uniforms were exchanged for white tropical kit, and 'Red Sea rig' was mandatory for evening wear and attendance in the Saloon for dinner.

Appendix B of P & O Regulations that referred in part to Cadets' quarters ('Cadets are to keep their quarters clean and tidy, and these will be inspected daily') proved onerous under the prevailing circumstances and akin to sweeping those famed Augean stables. However, encouraged by Company stricture to Commanders to encourage 'experiments' ('Commanders should encourage new ideas, and should regard themselves as defeated if the only objection they can make to some new idea is that it is never been done before') the Cadets prevailed upon the Chief Steward to donate some lengths of butter muslin, and the Chief Engineer some rubber grommet material, which when brought together were formed as soot filters over their cabin porthole; whilst almost totally excluding any air circulation in the monsoon heat of the Indian Ocean, the effect was at least to keep white uniform articles a little less grey, and the deck a little less crunchy.

The initial pattern of her voyage to those Cadets new to the Australian run conformed to past experience in that the Mediterranean's relatively equitable climate gave way to the dry heat of the Suez Canal, the sometimes heart-pumping proximity of heavy traffic through the confines of the Red Sea to Aden, followed by the haul to Colombo, in the island of Ceylon.

Thereafter, however, it was a 3,000 mile voyage to Fremantle, with only the Cocos Islands serving to break the monotony halfway towards Australia's western coastline. Except, of course, the Crossing of the Line ceremony, time honoured and well served by the canvas swimming pool into which the Captain allowed himself to be unceremoniously dunked, after others who were crossing for the first time had been appropriately initiated by a surrogate Neptune.

For at least one of the Cadets, however, the Australian coast was not to be the highlight of the voyage, albeit that for the first time visitor it was an eye-opener. As time was to eventually tell, Australia needed to be experienced to be properly appreciated rather than taken at initial face value, and *Pinjarra* was not the ship to open lines of communication, not being a regular trader to the country.

Horse riding there was to be along the beaches of Adelaide, and a never-to-be forgotten party at the house of friends, with the 'youngsters' consigned to the rumpus room for dancing. Here was a foretaste of colloquial differences, as one daughter of the house sought to secure the plug to the record player, bounced for the third time from its socket by wooden floor vibrations.

'Does any one here have Durex?' she enquired, and was momentarily encouraged by the involuntary movement of English hands towards breast pockets. Sellotape would have been better understood!

The Australian 'wharfies' demonstrated the industrial arrogance for which they were infamous, as well as a sense of humour that prevailed as long as it was not directed against themselves, but *Pinjarra* in a way was merely a means of transfer to a more exciting environment, and that was to take place just a few weeks after arriving on the Australian coast, but homeward bound.

As the funnel smoke curled lazily but steadily into the Cadets' quarters, and despite the crunching heat and underfoot soot particles, great excitement also pervaded, for news of some moment had reached the Captain via his Radio Officer, and eventually the Cadets, via the whistling Chief Officer.

Even as *Pinjarra*, née *Empire Paragon* creaked and undulated her way towards Aden, P & O London reached out with brief but precise instruction that her two senior Cadets were to prepare themselves for transfer to the liner *Strathaird*, she too being homeward bound from Australia, such transfer to take place within the furnace heat of Aden. No reason was given, at least not to the Cadets, and speculation was therefore rife. Transfer of one Cadet could be quickly rationalised by the death or injury of one of *Strathaird*'s officers, but the likelihood of two having been struck down simultaneously seemed extreme. An epidemic of some sort was rated as highly unlikely, but whatever it was, P & O was deemed fortunate to have two passenger-ship experienced Cadets so conveniently at hand, possessing among their uniform establishment No. 10 whites and Mess kit, ready and eager to fill the gaps caused by whatever catastrophe or quirk of fate had occurred.

Thoughts of promotion, albeit temporary, to Acting Junior Officer status were openly discussed and agreed as possible, and only the much earlier than planned settlement of bar bills seemed to present any sort of stumbling block to a smooth departure from *Pinjarra* (so sad, but duty calls) at Aden. It was deemed as unfortunate that the 'never-never' system of 'chitties', used universally through the P & O, was thus inconveniently short-stopped in its normal cycle of payment, rather like a sudden and unexpected foreclosure of a credit card facility. However, the Chief Steward was appeased by promise of payment upon his more pedestrian arrival at London, as, after all, the pay of an Acting Junior Officer would well cover any current shortfall.

As approach to Aden was made, so was the final packing of one's trunk completed, to ensure the final lid slam on cargo ship shorts and long white socks to emerge, chameleon like, wearing the correct rig for *Strathaird*. There would not be a lot of time for transfer, as *Strathaird* would be singled up ready for departure almost as *Pinjarra* rang off main engines, moored to her buoys.

Pinjarra entered Aden harbour, and dutifully dipped her Red to the White of the Royal Navy moored close to the harbour entrance, and then to the seniority of *Strathaird* as she was slowly passed, her high near-white sides surrounded by the bustle and scurry of launches returning passengers from shore purchasing excursions, and the last minute loading of Royal Mail, fresh water, and fuel oil from barges lying alongside. A thin trail of smoke from her single remaining funnel indicated that the liner was ready to proceed to sea, and indeed the Blue Peter flag flapped in desultory fashion from the Bridge halliards.

As *Pinjarra*'s port anchor clattered and splashed into Aden's harbour water, so she was nudged round to her mooring buoys by self-important jabbering tugs. The P & O launch came alongside to hasten the transfer of the two Cadets and their assorted baggage, her brasses glittering and twinkling in the harsh Yemen sunlight. Her seats were a dazzling white of scrubbed canvas cover and her crew, skilfully practised as any Naval ratings, were immaculate in their uniforms and boathook drill.

The two Cadets, already hotly uncomfortable in the more formal No. 10s whites of the passenger ship officer, but smartly correct with uniform cap, bade farewell to *Pinjarra* and took position on the pristine cleanliness of the white stern seats. Each had his sextant box upon his knees and looked with excitement towards *Strathaird*'s relative splendour across the sparkling flashing water of the harbour, her white hull and upperworks perhaps displaying just a trace of rust streak here and there as evidence of her voyage length. With a sharp order from the launch Tindal they were away from *Pinjarra*'s black hull and chugging towards *Strathaird* where much evidence of imminent departure was apparent.

A brief stop-off was made at the gangway of an Ellerman Line cargo ship to place her doctor aboard, and a small incident there underlined the myths that then surrounded P & O, and their continued perpetration.

Two Apprentices (Cadets) hung listlessly over the ship's rail close to the vessel's gangway head, clad only in dirty shorts and 'flip-flops', and covered in the unmistakable grime and rust particles that evidenced their recent employment; from which they took temporary respite judging by the newly lit cigarettes, and chipping hammers that lay waiting, close to hand. Below them in the sternsheets of the P & O launch sat the two immaculately uniformed Cadets, their Company cap badges, gold rising sun surmounting gold half prone anchor, clearly marking them as P & O, and their apprentice rank confirmed by the brief flash of vertical gold piping on each lapel.

A laconic drawled inquiry: 'What's life like in the Merchant Navy, bloke?' from the launch, where the opportunity had been seen as too good to miss, sponsored a swift and hostile response with strong Anglo-Saxon overtones. Only the immediate departure of the launch from the 'City Boat' gangway prevented the hurling of a chipping hammer, with scant regard for the consequences.

Arriving at *Strathaird*'s starboard side, the two Cadets, perspiring freely now in the constraints of uniform and the shimmering copper heat of Aden, scrambled up her high gangway, sextant boxes carefully carried and ready to take part in the vessel's position fixing routine as appropriate to anticipated watch-keeping as an Acting Junior Officer. They were met at the head of the gangway by the Chief Officer who looked decidedly harassed, askance at what he saw before him, but determined about something.

'Get down to your cabin on [he named the number and deck], get out of that bloody gear and into boilersuits, and report back to me here, at the double!'

'Yes, sir,' responded the more senior of the two lads in his soft but perceptible Australian accent. 'Can we borrow a couple of the crew to help get our trunks down below?'

The Chief Officer pulled his lips back from his teeth in a wolf-like grin, and with frustration bursting out all over shouted, 'Crew, boy, crew? You are the bloody crew!' and with that bombshell flung, raced off in pursuit of whatever.

Confirmation of this totally unexpected state of affairs came swiftly, as the two found four other Cadets scrambling into working gear in the eight-berth passenger cabin that had been temporarily allocated as Cadets' quarters, and the truth behind the circumstances gradually clarified.

Strathaird's Commander had been faced by an Indian Union ultimatum during the routine crew change in Bombay, which had apparently manifested itself in the new deck crew being physically restrained from joining the ship until Union officials had won improved service pay for their members, which really meant more pay-off for them.

Unprepared to have his command used as a negotiating pawn, the Captain simply sailed *Strathaird* from Bombay without a deck crew, thus in one fell stroke taking the wind from Union sails, and giving the ship's Purser and Medical Officers much needed practical seamanship experience at the same time. As far as the writer is aware, at no time before or since have P & O's doctors and Bureau staff actually lowered and hoisted gangways or worked the ship's ropes and mooring wires in a P & O liner, and a sterling effort they made of it too, under the expert eye of the Boatswain and his Boatswain's Mates. Stewards also were pushed into the breach and morale was never higher on board as the unthinkable was made to happen. Whether or not 122 Leadenhall Street, Headquarters of the P & O, had originally condoned the solution is not certain, but as an effective strike-breaking action, it was breathtakingly successful.

A follow-through to the action was the need to provide *Strathaird* with an effective deck crew presence, and to achieve this, the Company had concluded to deplete the cargo ship fleet of the necessary number of Cadets as quickly and as cost-effectively as possible. The six who joined in Aden were the first of the final eighteen Cadets that were to sail in *Strathaird*'s next voyage as her deck crew complement, their crewing activities strangely juxtaposed upon the continued need to continue their officer training, and their somewhat strained presence as active members of the Officers' Wardroom.

Strathaird, all gleaming white outside, was darkly wood-panelled inside, with a body odour of her own garnered through years of service, countless drums of polish and the lingering smell of human perspiration developed through time within the confines of her non-air-conditioned accommodation. She operated now as a one class vessel, devoted to tap the revenue generated by a flow of migrants to Australia, and whilst the traditions and standards of the P & O were unstintingly continued on board, it was obvious that no expensive facelift was scheduled for this old lady (built in 1932), but rather continued cosmetic touch-up as she faded quickly toward either a breaker's yard, or perhaps more ignominiously, conversion to a Greek island ferry. Factually, she was to be scrapped in Hong Kong in 1961, with part of her steel to be recycled into a housing complex.

Notwithstanding, the Boatswain (rather unusually moustached but not bearded) demonstrated fiercely that the loss of his deck Kalassis, Serang and Tindals would not reflect in depreciation of his responsi-

36. s.s Pinjarra, *deployed to the Australian trade 1957/58*

37. *s.s.* Strathaird

s.s. "STRATHAIRD"   23rd February, 1958.

B O M B A Y

          This circular is addressed primarily to the transit passengers
who were disappointed at being unable to visit the shore.

          The ship berthed alongside soon after 1 a.m., took fuel and water
and left the pier at 4 a.m. Those of you who were up at that time may have
heard and seen the crowd that was already gathering outside the gates. Had
the ship remained alongside any longer there would have been scenes of much
unpleasantness which would almost certainly have resulted in all our Goanese
Crew leaving the ship in anxiety. It would then have been very difficult
to sail the ship from Bombay, and, if at all, only at great discomfort to
all passengers. Anchoring off saved our crew from being intimidated, and
as a consequence we were able to sail only short of 8 Goanese and the Deck
Crew of 63 men. The alternative to this would have been to remain in
Bombay for an indefinite period while the dispute was settled. The former
Deck Crew had completed the term of their agreement and were persuaded by
their Union against any further extension of service. The new Deck Crew
had already signed their agreement to join the ship but were intimidated
ashore and prevented from joining. These men's main duties are routine
painting and maintenance of cargo gear, and their absence should not
affect passengers' comfort.

          While anchoring off saved a very ugly situation from developing,
it unfortunately prevented transit passengers from visiting the shore, as
there is insufficient suitable transport in the port. It is sincerely
appreciated what a great disappointment this was, but in the circumstances
no other course was open to us.

          Now a word about the background to the dispute.

          The P. & O. Company have employed Goanese as Cooks and Stewards
for over a hundred years. During all this time they have been loyal and
faithful servants in a Father to Son tradition, even in time of war which
by nationality was not their concern. In return for this service the
P. & O. have always paid a higher wage than other Shipping Companies.
Recently the Unions forced the shipping industry as a whole to increase
the level of wages to the P. & O. standard. Now, our men generally earn
the same wage as others, except in a few cases where our wage level is
still higher. In no case is it lower. Shortly after this the Unions
demanded the P. & O. to increase their wages by a further 10%. This, with
the support of the other Shipping Companies, the P. & O. refused to do.
Hence, the "strike", and you may gather the style and source of the
agitation from the demonstration and flag waving that took place while we
were at anchor.

          Bombay is not the only port, nor India the only country, where
labour disputes affect shipping, and it is hoped that this frank
explanation will put passengers more fully in the picture.

                        ---ooOoo---

38. Bombay circular

39. s.s. Strathaird 1958. Back row: Perry, Upjohn, Wesson, Lane. 2nd row: Trousdale, unknown, Graham, Hicks, Willi, Marsland, McLean. 3rd row: Cadet Officer Davie, Chief/O Cooke, Captain Perry, Staff Captain Cowen, 1st/O Hansing, Turner. 4th row: Tinsley, Harrington, Allan, Wilkin

40. *s.s.* Strathaird 1958. *Allan, Wilkin, Perry, Cadet Officer Davie, Harrington, Turner*

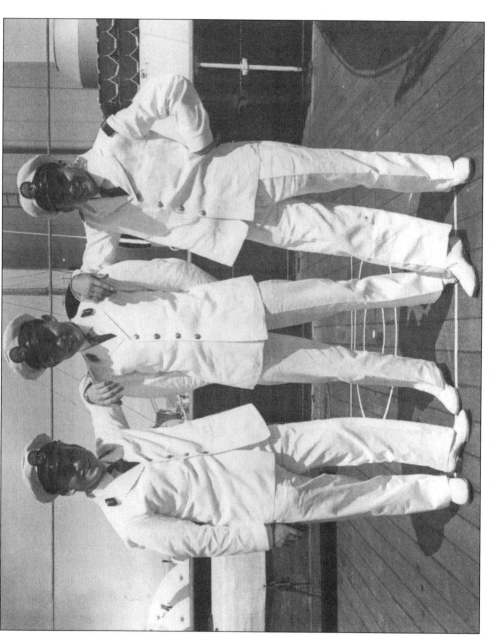

41. *s.s.* Strathaird 1958. Perry, Harrington, Cadet Officer Davie

P. & O. s.s.

"STRATHAIRD"

THE CADET OFFICER & CADETS

request the pleasure of the company of

....

at a Cocktail Party in the Wardroom

on Wednesday, 23rd April, at 6.15 p.m.

DRESS FORMAL

CARRIAGES AT 7.15 P.M.

42. *Invitation to cocktail party*

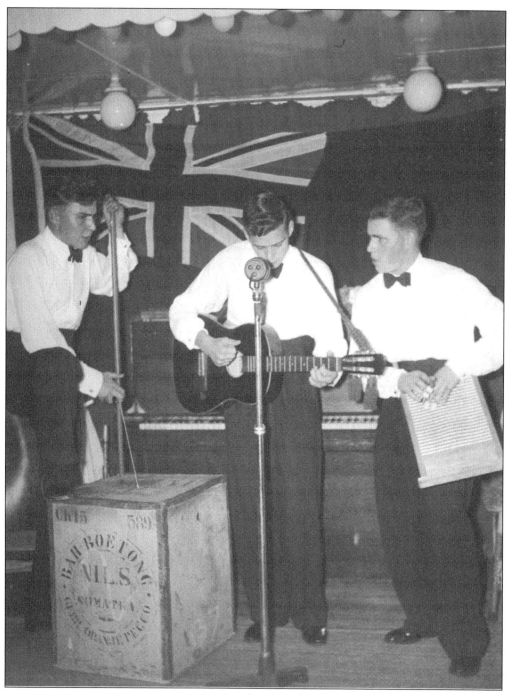

43. Skiffle group the 'Iberians', formed during Iberia's *cruise season 1957, reunited in* Strathaird *1958.*
Harrington, Davie, Perry

bility to keep the ship's passenger decks gleaming, the brasses shining, paint and varnish work immaculate and so forth, and with the exception of so-called 'topside work', which he steadfastly refused to allow Cadets to approach, he quickly established that this was not an unscheduled cruise season for the young gentlemen.

Ruefully amused at their own assumption to sudden status improvement, the six originals quickly flung their support behind him, determined to ensure that standards were upheld. By day, with turn-to at 0600 hours to achieve decks wash-down, they laboured until 1700 hours, at which time they cleaned up to become a possibly self-styled welcome addition in the evening to the dance floor in their freshly laundered mess kit. Their cabin became a meeting place during the day for young Australian and New Zealand girls intent on listening to their records and tapes, and it is a recorded fact that the Chief Officer, on finding eight such young females in what he believed to be the Cadets' cabin, briefly apologised for his unannounced intrusion.

'Very sorry,' he muttered on barging in unannounced, 'I thought this was the Cadets' cabin.'

In the act of confused withdrawal, he became aware of six uniform caps hanging on a row of hooks, and his frustration again evidenced itself.

'Damn it, this is the bloody Cadets' cabin,' he roared, reasserting his presence and authority. 'God only knows what it will be like when we get eighteen of the young bastards on board!' and slammed his way out to seek and then remonstrate with his young crew.

The six Cadets that joined *Strathaird* that late February 1958 in Aden became part of another adventure that marked her not unadventurous life, in that she had made an unscheduled stop-off in Djakarta en route from Australia, there to embark Dutch nationals and indigenous Indonesians as evacuees from the political upheaval that was Sukarno.

Strathaird's arrival at Rotterdam in a blinding, bitterly cold snowstorm was a delight in retrospect, as for the first time in their lives the Indonesians felt the wet touch of snow on their tropical skins, and danced delightedly through the little powdery drifts that scurried, wind driven, across the ship's wooden decking. The Dutch, thoughtfully practical as in most things, had provided each of their colonial guests with brightly coloured tracksuits, and the drabness of a wintertime passage through the Maas to Rotterdam docks was livened by the infectious excitement and surge of colour thus provided by the Indonesians as they 'came home'.

From Aden to Rotterdam however was a time of adjustment for the Cadets, as they fell into the mixed routine of working for the Boatswain or standing Bridge Watches during close-coasting sectors of the voyage. It was also the opportunity to see at close quarters another of P & O's 'character' Captains, for *Strathaird*'s Captain was all of that, displaying at times an eccentricity that endeared him to most, and amazed not a few.

His quarters, situated just below the Bridge, were imposingly wood panelled and furnished as befitted the Captain of a P & O liner, and into this holy of holies stepped nervously one of his newly joined Cadets, acting as messenger from the Officer of the Watch that paced the Bridge deck above.

Passing the bathroom on his right, he approached through a short, carpeted passage toward the lounge from where 'come in, come in,' sounded again, this time displaying some brief impatience. Cap tucked correctly under left arm and nervous at this first direct encounter, the Cadet tendered the message from the Bridge, and waited in respectful and awe-struck silence.

Glancing up from under white haired eyebrows, and with his unique gold P & O braid of rank twinkling from the shoulders of his white uniform jacket, the Captain broke the silence.

'What's your name, Cadet?' he enquired. The Cadet responded with his surname.

'That's strange, so's mine,' ruminated the Captain, 'and where are you from then?'

'Eastbourne, sir, in Sussex,' the Cadet replied.

'How very odd, that's my hometown too. Are we related, do you think?'

'N–not that I'm aware of, sir,' replied the Cadet alarmed at the coincidence and indeed the length of exposure to Deity, and fled quickly at the now absent-minded nod of dismissal as the Captain turned his attention elsewhere.

'You've been a bloody long time,' growled the First Officer, as the Cadet returned to the Bridge, his bark always infinitely worse than his bite, and at that brought *Strathaird* round to her new course with a laconic but precise order to the Quartermaster, the Third Officer on the Bridge wing quickly memorising his three 'fix' bearings and moving swiftly to mark the ship's position to chart.

Strathaird's Commander, like most of his generation of P & O Captains, liked to show passengers points of interest wherever possible during what, at times, was a boringly uneventful day of passage. This often took the form of passing close to other P & O liners or cargo ships, which became quite exciting as sirens boomed and cried to each other across a sometimes alarmingly short stretch of maelstromed water, and ensigns snapped and cracked at their halliards as they dipped and rose in respectful salute.

Close coasting was always of interest to passengers too, and whether true or not, it was accepted by most that some Captains vied with others to achieve the closest pass to certain headlands, their Officers of the Watch nail chewing their continuous 'fixes' to the chart, adrenalin reassuring worried minds that 'that old man knows what he's doing'.

Cape St Vincent, the south-easterly extremity of Portugal, was such a point of interest as homeward bound ships, flushed to the waters of the North Atlantic from the Strait of Gibraltar, turned north, and so it was with *Strathaird* as eight bells of the 4-8 watch approached, and St Vincent's great light flashed out from the white painted lighthouse no longer visible in the swift befallen darkness. Passengers crowded the starboard rails and exclaimed at the sound of waves crashing on St Vincent's forefoot, and officers pondered the wisdom of such massive adjacence as the light described its pre-ordained track above *Strathaird*'s mast tops.

'Damned charts,' remonstrated the Captain to no one in particular as he formally handed the ship's con back to the Officer of the Watch, 'if they'd only bring them up to date we could have gone a damned sight closer!' It was to the Hydrographer of the Navy that silent thanks were given, at his wisdom and forethought in not deploying his meagre resources to the re-charting of Cape St Vincent.

To be entertained to cocktails in the Captain's quarters before dinner was a much sought-after privilege by passengers, the occasion being one of some pomp and circumstance with the Captain and his senior officers in formal mess kit and the male passengers invariably in black tie order with their ladies suitably clad in evening gowns.

Stewards hovered with canapés on silver salvers, and discreetly ensured that glasses were refilled, while the muted hum of polite small talk was occasionally livened by a quick snap of laughter as humour became emboldened by Gordons or Bells.

Arrival to such soirées in *Strathaird*, however, was different. Quite different. Among the Captain's prized possessions was a long-barrelled brass pea-shooter, manufactured for him by an Engineer Officer, and as passengers were escorted by his servant from door to reception area, they would receive stinging whip of projectile pea on exposed areas, puffed thereto from behind the curtained doorway of the Captain's bathroom. Rarely challenged by his visitors (who would believe them anyway?) his was a peccadilo that offered no harm, but great amusement to those that were aware.

Officers and Cadets were allowed to use the after-end of *Strathaird*'s Bridge deck for sun bathing during off-duty hours, a privilege well appreciated by those intent on a few hours of peace away from the constant demands of passengers. In the quiet heat of the afternoon, it was not unusual, however, to feel the sudden sharp splat of split-pea against perspiring skin, and to recognise the white haired perpetrater of this sudden offence as the Captain skipped quickly back into hiding behind the yellow funnel casing or adjacent ventilator hoods. As a Cadet, and glancing swiftly round at fellow sun-worshippers seeking confirmation of the phenomenon, it was prudent to pretend that it had never happened. After all, everyone else did.

Strathaird's eventual arrival back in London brought relief of a sort to the Boatswain, hard-pressed as he was to keep the ship up to P & O standards of appearance with such a small working complement. The Chief Officer, whilst welcoming the thought of more hands, showed occasional signs of deep apprehension that his Cadet complement was at least to double.

In fact, *Strathaird* was to sail from London's odious river to Australia with sixteen Cadets, although 'Personnel' at 122 Leadenhall St. had thoughtfully placed a further Cadet, almost out of 'Indentures', in charge as Cadet Officer. So, seventeen in all, and unique in the history of the P & O passenger fleet. Even Mr Errington could not have foreseen such an event, and the bespoke tailors rallied quickly round to kit out those among the young gentlemen who had yet to sail in passenger ships. Not entirely windfall profit, however, as even P & O recognised the unique circumstances, and mindful of the need for uniformity, issued each Cadet with standard naval blue working rig, without charge.

By sheer coincidence, but of imminent social value to the ship's voyage, the three Cadets that had formed the 'Iberians' skiffle group during the past cruising season found themselves together again with, most appropriately, the Cadet Officer still leading!

The RNVR Club in Hill Street, London maintained several 'cabins' for officer members visiting town, and one of *Strathaird*'s Cadets, as a Midshipman RNR, had been fortunate enough to secure himself a berth for the night, prior to rejoining the ship after a few days' leave. The Cadet Officer, a friend of long-standing since *Cannanore* days, had offered to collect him en route to Tilbury, his father in turn having generously loaned his black Wolseley saloon for the carriage of kit. Arriving promptly as arranged before the Club's imposing portals, a navy blue half duffle jacket covering his braid of rank, the Cadet Officer was, with some hauteur, instructed by the porter to load 'the gentleman's suitcases to the car,' and to wait.

'Your driver is waiting your convenience, sir,' he politely intoned, and scarcely able to keep a straight face the Cadet took his seat in the car. Fortunately good humour transcended initial indignation, and the Cadet Officer played out the charade until clear of the Club entrance, and Hill Street was left behind midst shouts of laughter.

Strathaird's 'Board of Trade Sports', the demonstration of a British Merchantman's ability to properly utilise life-saving equipment, was this time different, and much remarked by P & O's Marine Superintendent as he worried his way round with 'Officialdom', in Tilbury. That he too might have forgotten that a P & O Cadet was trained to perform seamanlike functions was unthinkable, but his demeanor certainly indicated such a memory lapse. Only successful completion of the 'Sports' gave cause for belated acknowledgement, and a grudging admission that perhaps *Strathaird* would survive the ordeal, sans Indian crew. Obviously encouraged, he addressed the paraded Cadets, and Nelson-like encouraged them to do their duty, not for Country, but for Company! Several blind eyes would thereafter require to be used, particularly by the Chief Officer, but it was to be proved that the Cadets would well earn their keep.

The seventeen Cadets were berthed in cabins on 'E' deck, forward of what used to be the First Class Restaurant, in her heyday. The restaurant retained still the 1930s decor as popular with the 'Strath' clan of vessel, but catered now largely for low fare, one class passengers, migrants to Australia. This adjacence to passenger accommodation, as in the *Iberia*, was a source of constant worry to the much put upon Chief Officer, but in this case it seemed to be that the 'safety in numbers' maxim worked as a bromide – either that, or the daily work schedule imposed by the Boatswain found most Cadets too exhausted at the day's end to do much else than droop, particularly in the stifling heat of *Strathaid*'s non-air-conditioned interior.

By and large, however, the dual roles expected of the Cadets, lascar by day and social young officers in the evenings, placed by their sheer volume considerable strain upon the ship's officers' social structure.

This was most vociferously remarked by the Engineer Officers, who felt that the Cadets should not even be granted Wardroom membership, as they were effectively employed as deckhands. This was naturally protested by the Cadets themselves, who fell into the unfortunate trap of comparing their own officer training (pre-sea as well as afloat) to that of apprentices from British Rail who had merely bought an Engineer Officer's uniform. Despite the union-like pedantry displayed by the boiler maker, self-appointed spokesman for the Engineer Officers, compromise was achieved by the Chief Officer in his capacity as Wardroom President. Only a defined number of Cadets would be free to use the Wardroom itself at any one time, and Cadet attendance to a dance or fancy dress ball night would be restricted to four.

It was probably at this time that undiplomatic reference was aired to the usually unspoken suggestion that a ruckus created by Deck Officers (and Cadets by extension) was high-spirits, whereas by Engineers it was hooliganism!!

For the occasion of the first dance attendance, the four most senior Cadets were put forward, largely for their previous experience in passenger liners during the cruising seasons. Critical inspection of their appearance was made by the Cadet Officer, and happy that white mess jackets were immaculate, black bows correctly tied, and shoes highly polished the *pièce de resistance* was brought out. Between the seventeen Cadets they had managed to muster four pairs of white dress gloves!

Thus as *Strathaird* gently rolled her way beneath the Mediterranean skies towards Port Said, the four young gentlemen solemnly danced the night away, taking infinite pains to seek partners among the older or more matronly of the female passengers. Not unnaturally, this Cinderella type role had its pumpkin hour, and whilst no glass dress-shoes remained behind, did not one white glove turn back into a white mouse?

The Engineers were incensed, and indeed the Chief Officer had perforce to admonish and ban such further attempts at upstaging. His put-down was much tempered however by his reference to remarks passed by one of his dance partners the previous evening.

'How much more pleasant it is to dance with one of the Cadets – they've solved the problem of perspiring hands on the back!'

As the temperature and humidity increased with passage through the Suez Canal, Red Sea and Indian Ocean so did the degree of wonder that the ship's band (or 'prickly heat quartet' as they were affectionately known) could continue to play in tune. How could the violin strings not be affected by the ever dampening heat, or the perspiration that globuled perpetually from forehead to nose to chin?

Tempers too became somewhat temperature frayed, not least of all for the Cadets at meal times, where a quick change from deck-work gear to No. 10 white uniform in the tropics had to be made at breakfast and lunch, prior to eating in the passenger restaurant. Having 'turned to' between 0600 and 0800 to wash down decks (as often as not a means of reducing the ship's temperature) pressure to get showered and changed (with limited fresh water facilities) before breakfast was intense, and usually noisy. Added to this was the ex-laundry state of the No. 10 white uniforms (board hard, with trouser legs seemingly glued together with starch) which would bring Cadets to the breakfast table looking like a perspiring Tin Man of Oz, and short on fuse. This fuse was often lit by Alphonso!

In common with all P & O ships *Strathaird* carried a large complement of Goanese stewards, although it is probably fair to say that if there was any choice available to P & O, the brighter and more proficient would probably have been appointed to other than the 'Straths' at that stage of their employment.

Alphonso (if that was indeed his name), despite his good humour and past record, should definitely have been retired. As it was, the Restaurant Chief Steward, seeing a way to keep Alphonso away from passengers, put him to serve at the Cadets' table.

Beaming benignly, his steward's white jacket always besmeared and undone at the neck, and with ear hair standing bushily to the horizontal, he would take breakfast orders. He would never ever get them right!

'But I ordered fruit juice, Alphonso.'

'Yes, sahib, cornflakes.'

'I ordered fried eggs, Alphonso.'

'Yes, sahib, fish kedgeree.'

'Are these cornflakes the fish I ordered, Alphonso?'

'Yes, sahib, cornflakes.'

Too much for one Cadet one hot, steamingly humid morning, and with suspicions of prickly heat beneath the freshly laundered highly starched trousers, he pushed back his chair from the table and rose stiffly to his feet. The upward movement was only momentarily delayed by a tackiness on the seat, and glancing down with dawning horror, he saw on the shiny green leather almost a spoonful of marmalade, without doubt dropped there by the redoubtable Alphonso.

'Alphonso,' he roared, placing one foot on the chair, 'there's bloody marmalade all over this chair.'

'Yes, sahib, marmalade,' responded Alphonso, pleased to have got one order apparently right.

At this the Cadet stormed from the restaurant, giving fellow-Cadets and breakfasting migrants full view of his retreating uniform, liberally covered in the posterior area by copious amounts of Chivers Thick Cut! One indignant migrant, thickly from the North of England, addressed a complaint to the Staff Captain about the outrageous attitude adopted by Cadets to the native servants, and one such Cadet duly and properly received admonishment.

For all that *Strathaird* was, according to one author, 'the pride of the P & O fleet relegated to one class low fare sailings', the restaurant fare was pretty good, as evidenced by the Fancy Dress Ball Dinner Menu of 24 April 1958.

Grapefuit au Marashimo
Consomme Grimaldi
Cream Solferino

Lemon Sole Fillets, Cambridge Sauce
Baked Sugar Ham Marsala
Chicken Saute Chausseur

Potatoes
Rissolees
Nature
Runner Beans

Cold Sideboard
Haunch of Lamb
Yale Pie
Terrine of Hare
Salade Grande Dutchess

Sweets
Sherry Trifle
Coupe Clecquot
Dates
Figs
Assorted Nuts

Alphonso's Cadets would have enjoyed it immensely, not unlike a mystery tour! Not bad either, for a migrant ship!

The daily repetition of washing down decks and paintwork became truly monotonous, and the sanding of wooden handrails an exercise in boredom. The uniform working gear, so generously handed out by 122 Leadenhall St., proved in the tropics to be uncomfortably hot and sticky and with fresh water washing facilities in passenger accommodation at a premium, contributory to much dhobi itch. Shorts were not permitted within the dress code, and with their cabins deep within her non-airconditioned interior, the Cadets found the days to be largely tedious and the nights uncomfortably hot.

Some of the Greek migrants, en route to Melbourne, demonstrated either their ignorance or their flexibility in the matter of clothes washing, in that they concluded the urinals were for this purpose!

Aware of close and humid condition below decks, P & O kept stocks of camp beds for the use of passengers. It was no unusual sight at early morning wash-down to see passengers scurrying out of the way of the salt water jets as they avoided the swish and slurp of the hard brushes and squeegees flung hither and thither by bleary eyed Cadets.

Perhaps more unusual was the Cadet's report made to the Officer of the Watch whilst *Strathaird* lay at anchor in the Bitter Lakes of the Suez Canal. Having completed his rounds of the decks (precautionary to ensure no unwelcome 'boarders' from the so-called bum boats) he advised the First Officer that two lesbians had been sighted on the Boat Deck.

'What do you mean, lesbians?' enquired the First Officer.

'You know, Sir, two women,' replied the Cadet.

'I know what blasted lesbians are,' retorted the Watch Officer impatiently, 'but how do you know they are lesbians?' he concluded.

'Because they're performing on the Boat Deck,' came the assured reply.

Without further ado, the First Officer concluded that a more serious overview was properly appropriate, and departed from the Bridge at a fast clip, towards the area of reported activity.

'He's bloody right,' he confirmed to his Junior Watch Officer on his breathless return to the Bridge, and the Third Officer in his turn left to view this odd form of matins. By early morning wash-deck time they had departed, and in so doing had avoided the proverbial 'bucket of cold water' treatment from the thin blue line of advancing Cadets.

Wash deck hoses served another purpose on that voyage. Instructed by the Chief Officer to ensure that no 'bum-boat' traders boarded at Port Said, the Cadet Officer proceeded to the after gangway deck with several stalwarts from among his Cadet team – there to find that some thirty traders had already boarded, and were in the process of laying out their stalls on the deck. Singling out the most prominent, a large Egyptian who sported the unlikely trade name of 'Jock McGregor', the Cadet Officer informed him that they would have fifteen minutes to clear the ship, or 'otherwise take the consequences'.

The Egyptian thought this to be a great joke, and laughingly passed the message to his fellow traders who joined him in humoured dismissal of the threat, and continued to establish their beach-head, with more set to join them from the boats. Physically outnumbered, the Cadet Officer was not to be out-manoeuvred.

'Ten more minutes!' he shouted, and at that the Cadets began connecting up wash-deck hoses to the high pressure salt water outlets in the ring system.

More puzzled than apprehensive, the portly purveyor of toy stuffed camels gave an expansive smile and clucked chidingly at this display of upstart lack of understanding. Hands outstretched, he advanced to reassure them that their presence would cause no problems.

'Five more minutes,' intoned the Cadet Officer, and glanced pointedly at his wristwatch.

The slow and resentful withdrawal of traders and goods to the boats turned into a mad scramble as the ring-main valves were opened a turn, and tepid salt water gave a restrained short leap to the deck, as unequivocal as a warning shot across a bow.

Migrant passengers would later lodge a complaint about the 'cavalier attitude' of the Cadets, and they appeared unwilling to understand that the continued presence of the traders on board would have resulted in much pilferage and theft from passenger cabins. Notwithstanding, it was a welcome change in the routine use of hoses!

Arrival at an Australian port in a P & O liner in the 50s was an exciting affair, with literally hundreds of citizens turning out to witness the event, if not to meet relatives joining them from their 'home country'. Long haul air-travel was not routinely established and the liners represented for most the tenuous connection to their land of birth, and indeed the most likely mode of travel thereto.

It was always emotional, and to the young Cadets seeing it for the first time, a moving experience. Equally moving were the shouts of encouragement or anguish from the Boatswain and his mates, or the officers at stations fore and aft, as the young crew strived to improve their handling of the wire springs and large manila headropes that snugged *Strathaird* to Australian soil.

Fremantle first, in Western Australia, then round Cape Leewen to Adelaide in South Australia, having traversed that fickle water, the Australian Bight. Thereafter to Melbourne in the State of Victoria, followed by transit of the Bass Strait between Victoria and Tasmania, before turning north to Sydney in the State of New South Wales. For these Cadets new to the Australian coast, there was a chance to test the truth in the suggestion that:

In Fremantle they ask	'What will you have?'
In Adelaide	'What church do you attend?'
In Melbourne	'What school do you go to?'
In Sydney	'What business are you in?'

The tale continues to Brisbane where it was suggested the question asked is in counterpoint to that of Fremantle namely: 'Would you like the other half?' *Strathaird* did not go that far north, but in general the suggestion appeared to be valid.

In between washing decks, paintwork, boat deck screen windows and other tasks of an onerous nature, the 'Iberians' continued to practise their musical craft to the probable degree that a cult following on board was not entirely out of the question. Guitar, washboard and tea-chest bass accompanied by three voices in melodious conjunction brought pleasure to many, and indeed was brought to a tumultuous climax on the occasion of *Strathaird*'s Sydney Ball, where the group appeared in cabaret!

The Sydney Ball was part of P & O tradition, and every liner, during the few days secured alongside in Sydney, would indulge several hundred guests to the ship to a taste of opulent life aboard. Dinner jackets were of course mandatory, and no lady would be seen in anything less than full ballgown. To be invited was a social achievement of no small note, and the strains of the ship's orchestra would mix the patterns and colours of Australian *haute couture* with white sharkskin tuxedos to the wee small hours of a Sydney morning. That the *Strathaird* had the 'Iberians' to bring greater sophisticated depth to the occasion was a coup for the Wardroom secretary to whom fell the task of organisation, and they were warmly received.

Arcadia had a similar such event in Sydney some years later, and midnight rounds by the Officer of the Watch brought firm evidence of the quality of guests who attended. Noticing that the Wardroom door was slightly ajar, he poked his head round the door to check that the bar grill was properly secure. From behind the green leather sofa, in dulcet female Australian tone came the immortal words:

'Where's yer manners! Tits first, yer dirty bastard!'

Such was the 'Iberians' success that an invitation was received to audition for a Sydney television show! This too went well, and the producer enthusiastically indicated that upon the vessel's return to Sydney the following voyage, the 'Iberians' would have a spot on his show. Regrettably, Personnel in Leadenhall Street had other ideas, for upon *Strathaird*'s return to London, the bass player was reassigned to another vessel, as were several other Cadets, as P & O began to infiltrate a proper crew back onto *Strathaird*.

The group was also asked to play on one of Sydney's radio stations (was the programme called 'Rumpus Room'?) but regrettably the person being interviewed before them, the head of MGM, over-ran his time, and their chance was lost. There was much disappointment aboard *Strathaird* with all radios tuned to that particular station, but it was not to be.

'Mind the door, mate!' shouted the driver of the Holden taxi as a frustrated Cadet slammed out of his car.

'If it can take your driving, it can stand its bloody door being slammed,' came the snarled response, with sufficient intensity to dissuade the cabby from including in the usual 'pommy bastard' rejoinder!

For those Cadets visiting the Australian coast for the first time, the Australian penchant for referring to Brits as Poms was puzzling, and seemed to have no likely explanation. Vague references to cheek colouring resembling pomegranates did not seem to sustain any sort of scrutiny, and no plausible ideas came from the Australians themselves, particularly those of Mediterranean origin of which there were many.

It was the entrepreneurial activities of the four Cadets of *Patonga* some years later that, by chance, came up with the answer. They had purchased a Holden car in Fremantle, its presence on board *Patonga* allowed by the Captain only on the clear understanding that its movement from hatch top to wharf and vice versa was undertaken wholly by the Cadets. A training exercise no less, in rigging derricks, driving winches and securing cargo slings. Who said P & O did not properly train Cadets!

That apart, they covered expenses by hiring it out to the officers, and on this particular occasion, it had served as transport from Beauty Point to Port Arthur in Tasmania, site of one of Australia's first penal settlements. There in the museum, carefully preserved, were examples of deportation orders served on certain hapless folk, often for such offences as 'stealing a cambric handkerchief' or somesuch. Across each deportation order were stamped the initials P.O.M.E., abbreviation for 'Prisoner of Mother England'. Which in itself inspired the question as to who should call who 'Poms'.

The P & O experiment in crewing was drawing to a close, and not many weeks separated *Strathaird*'s Cadets from dispersal to other units of the P & O fleet. However, there was the homeward voyage, and that was as different as chalk to cheese to the outward migrant leg. The 'Straths' were popular with the young, and *Strathaird* was to have her full complement of young Australian and New Zealand people on board, intent on fully exploiting the time between leaving the Australian coast and arrival at England's fair shores.

To suggest that the Chief Officer's worst fears were realised is probably an understatement, as the Cadets threw themselves enthusiastically into the business of hosting when not scrubbing or polishing. The homeward voyage was therefore all too short, but suffice it to say, a happy one!

For the three months and twenty days that *Strathaird* was home to her Cadet crew, the staid old lady came alive, and if ships can be said to twinkle, she twinkled! She returned to London a little more dishevelled, perhaps, than would have been normal with a full crew complement, but with panache!

A certain kind of madness had prevailed, encouraged no doubt by a Captain who puffed split peas at puzzled passengers, and epitomised by such as the Assistant Surgeon, a burly Scot with ever a smile. He would receive his pre-dinner cocktail guests to his cabin immaculate to the waist in Officer's Mess-kit, but unusually attired waist down in an Indian lungi! To the unsuspecting Woman Assistant Purser (who wore a black tie as part of her uniform) he would ask, 'Do you want that tie?'

'Yes,' would come the puzzled response.

'Well, here you are then,' he would rejoin, snipping through the tie at the knot with his surgical scissors, and handing the remains to the stricken girl.

The more seasoned tried the response 'No,' only to see the severed portion tossed to the floor with the words: 'Very well then, let's throw it away!'

It was a singular experience for all who sailed in *Strathaird* those months, and for the Cadets, unforgettable! Built in 1932 by Vickers Armstrong in Barrow, and sister to *Strathnaver*, *Strathmere*, *Stratheden* and the war demised *Strathallan*, she was to be finally retired in June 1961. One of her Cadets was honoured to serve as Third Officer on *Canberra*'s maiden voyage. The two ships passed at sea on 8 June 1961, *Canberra* outward bound on her maiden voyage, and *Strathaird* flying her paying off pennant homeward bound, and neither of the Commanders could have felt anything but immense pride!

However, in that June of 1958, pushing upstream through the turgid waters of the Thames toward Tilbury, she had still some way to go! She was moreover to do it thereafter without the aid of Cadets, as for those aboard who handled *Strathaird*'s headropes, stern ropes and springs for the last time, Personnel of Leadenhall Street had already made plans.

'I do believe, Sir,' murmured Mr Errington discreetly to two of *Strathaird*'s Cadets, 'you should anticipate appointment to *Arcadia*'s cruise programme in ten days' time.'

CHAPTER 14

Mediterranean Cruising: *Arcadia*

A S HER SISTER-SHIP *Iberia* took shape in Belfast, so did *Arcadia* similarly grow from keel to truck, but in the Clydebank yard of John Brown. Each entered service in 1954, and they were virtually indistinguishable one to the other in scantling, save that *Arcadia* grossed at 29,734 tons compared to *Iberia*'s 29,614 tons and at 722 ft in length she could only claim three feet additional to her sister.

The greatest visible difference lay in their funnel constructions, *Arcadia* sporting a domed funnel with a distinctive black top whereas *Iberia*'s funnel had a round grated facing to the front with no break in the buff colour other than the occasional soot pattern. A less obvious difference was that *Arcadia*'s illuminated name signs were directly at the base of the funnel casing, whereas those of *Iberia* were sited abaft the funnel.

To the six Cadets joining *Arcadia* for the cruising season, however, she was little different from *Iberia* in her thin patina of Tilbury grime, and for each this brought about a feeling of *déjà vu*, heightened for one by other aspects. He had served in *Iberia* the previous year, and *Arcadia*'s accommodation and public rooms were almost identical, with the Cadets quartered yet again on 'D' deck right outside the First Class restaurant.

'Welcome aboard, bloke,' said Simon, and the feeling of *déjà vu* was complete! Simon, birdman of the *Cannanore*, and dispenser of much Guinness in *Iberia* the previous year, was serving as Cadet Officer in *Arcadia*! That he was able to demonstrate leadership in this capacity to his fellow cruising Cadets was instantly in doubt, and he would for the rest of the cruising season have to live with the fact that at least two Cadets were his senior, albeit that he wore the shoulder braid of the P & O Officer. Personnel had slipped up, but in the general scheme of things it mattered little.

P & O passenger ships did not employ the services of ordained Ministers, the Captain or Staff Captain conducting Sunday services at sea. The newly joined Stenographer (Female Assistant Purser) and

160

Children's Hostess were not aware of this however, and submitted willingly to be interviewed by one of the six Cadets posing as the Ship's Padre, complete with manufactured 'dog collar' to lend appropriate gravitas! The season was beginning!

Arcadia's cruise programme was broadly the same as *Iberia*'s had been the previous year, albeit that it was one month shorter. It also included a so-called 'Northern Cities Cruise', where as a change from the traditional limpid summer heat of the Mediterranean, *Arcadia* sailed east thence north from Southampton towards Scandinavia to transit the Skagerrak, the Kattegat and so eventually to Finland.

However, for the Cadets, much preparation and training in the passenger launches had again to be entered into, for some breaking new ground and for others as refresher activity. Tilbury yet again witnessed the turgid dock waters churned by the swift passage of the 'limousines' as Cadets put both themselves and their craft through their paces, or the more stately progress of the 'penny buses'.

Despite warnings and advice from 'old hands' of previous cruising experience, the metal gangways lowered to the waterline for practice purposes crashed resoundingly against the ship's white hull as inexperienced coxswains practised the art of coming alongside. A speed wake demonstrated yet again that the dashing approach circle culminating in a full reverse dead stop bang alongside the gangway platform was almost guaranteed to distress passengers and Chief Officers, and indeed the ship's carpenters told off to repair the gangway damage!

The Chief Officer, risen and established now from the rusty black hull of *Pinjarra*, expounded the theory that for all boats to be lowered simultaneously from the boat deck to water not only would expedite the movement of passengers ashore, but would also impress passengers in its seamanlike execution. Tried and tested in the flat calm of Tilbury dock it did appear in practice to hold considerable merit and was therefore planned for the first Mediterranean boat port.

Proficient at their appointed task the Cadets did become, however, and as always the P & O Port Superintendent eventually and grudgingly agreed that passengers, that most cosseted source of P & O revenue, would be safely and professionally ferried to and from the ship as she lay offshore at anchor under the hot Mediterranean sun. This season, the Port of Split in the then Yugoslavia was to test those skills to the full.

Aside from the boating and social aspects of a Cadet's life aboard the cruising liners, Chief Officers felt it encumbent upon them to instill into their charges other facets of training that would contribute to their eventual passing of the Second Mate's Certificate. To this end, the once whistling Chief Officer of ex *Pinjarra* fame concluded that, between boat ports, the Cadets should paint out one of *Arcadia*'s cargo rooms, empty now but usually filled with such as mail bags during the vessel's normal employment on the Australian run.

In the event, and as bonus to their learning curve, the Cadets were exposed to a small piece of social and political history. Carefully chalked onto one bulkhead by an Australian 'wharfie' was his opinion of the then Prime Minister of Australia, Sir Robert Gordon Menzies, which these pages will attempt to immortalise as hereunder:

Bob Menzies – french letter on the penis of progress!'

Yugoslavia was a popular destination for the cruise liners, and once through the Messina Strait (night passage marked by the 10 inch signalling lamp being trained from the ship's bridge wing on the overhead cables), course was set north-east through the Ionian Sea to the Adriatic, and thence to Dubrovnik on the Dalmatian Coast. Founded in AD 639 by refugees from the Graeco-Roman colony of Epidaurum, its passage through history has been beset by events that forced walls and fortresses to be built to enclose the town, whilst imposed cultures from Rome and Venice, Hungary, Croatia and Napoleon's Paris produced monuments that reflect the vitality of her existence during thirteen centuries.

It was therefore entirely appropriate that he who had instilled history in *Conway*'s Cadets should choose to take holiday that year in Dubrovnik, the Master steeping himself in the past that existed within the thick walls, and not a little of the local plum brandy!

Arcadia's starboard anchor cleaved into the clear sparkling waters of the anchorage to the east of Dubrovnik and the cable clattered and rattled its way past the compressors, to the ordained length that would have the vessel brought up comfortably facing into the slight prevailing breeze.

On the Bridge, the Chief Officer, immaculately dressed in crisp white uniform, saw that his Cadets were ready, and gave the signal for the boats to be launched. Serangs and Tindals, themselves colourfully attired in best uniforms, lifted the davit brake handles and one by one the 'limousines' and 'penny buses' sped down the ship's high white hull to land with satisfying splash and surge into the Adriatic.

The practised hands of the Indian seamen at bow and stern disengaged the lifting blocks and the Cadets brought their boats away from the ship's side to await the final rigging of pontoons under the slender gangways. By this time, a simultaneous launching of all boats had been reluctantly abandoned by the Chief Officer. At the first practical attempt, the Mediterranean swell although slight had been sufficient to cause all boats to mêlée together once in the water, to the high embarrassment of Cadets and much applause from passengers crowding the ship's rails for the show.

The first 'limousine' to speed shorewards was coxed by the only ex-*Conway* Cadet aboard *Arcadia*, and coincidentally he had not only listened in awe to the wartime exploits of Humph the Desert Rat at *Conway*, but had also aspired to the cricket team. Carefully he brought his launch into the designated passenger landing place that was crowded with curious holiday makers, and with a short burst of stern power, brought the craft alongside. To look from the boat's small Bridge to the twitching moustache surmounting the broad friendly grin of the Desert Rat came as a pleasurable surprise. To show the historian over *Arcadia* shortly thereafter was a proud interlude, and an invitation to join the Master for a plum brandy ashore a pleasing acknowledgment of progress from *Conway* days.

From Dubrovnik *Arcadia* steamed leisurely further north to Split, another so-called boating port, and the now routine process of moving passengers between the ship and shore excursions proceeded routinely through the hot still day, *Arcadia* lying to anchor about a mile offshore.

'Limousines' and 'penny buses' growled and chugged their furrows back and forth, whilst knees and forearms, those parts of Cadets' anatomy exposed by uniform tropical shorts, long socks and short sleeved shirts, reddened or browned as the case may be. Mother Nature, however, bored by the monotonous tranquillity of it all, took a hand in the day's events, concluding to have one of her sudden summer wind storms that can sweep onto the Dalmatian coast with startling force.

The timing was bad for as the weather deteriorated, so the bulk of passengers arrived back from their day's excursions, eager to return to the air-conditioned comfort of *Arcadia* and her many inviting bars. Additionally, *Arcadia*'s Commander wisely concluded that as his command now lay off a lee shore, prudence dictated that she be moved further offshore. The distance between ship and shore therefore doubled as sea conditions deteriorated, and it was quickly to become apparent that the 'limousines' were not good sea-boats, whereas the 'penny buses' were exceptional.

The passengers loved it in the main, as a diversion from a normal cruising day, and with their faith in the Cadets' ability total, saw little to fear from the situation. On the ship, however, the Captain, Staff Captain, Chief Officer and Officer of the Watch peered anxiously through binoculars as sea-conditions worsened. The Cadet coxswains eased throttles back to prevent their craft taking water as they pitched and rolled their passenger-laden way towards the ship, their task made much more difficult by the necessary withdrawal of the large boat pontoon normally secured beneath the gangways.

The Cadet Officer's limousine was the first casualty, he perhaps having been less prudent than others in reducing his craft's speed. 'She's sinking,' came the terse observation. Indeed, the limousine had taken so much water aboard that the engine compartment was flooded, and the boat lay dead in the water, her upperworks only occasionally showing through the waves.

About to leave the gangway for another trip to shore, one of the two senior-most Cadets was directed to take his 'penny bus' to the rescue, and empty of passengers, he proceeded apace to the stricken craft. It wallowed with water up to the gunwales inside, the boat being prevented from sinking only by her buoyancy tanks, thoughtfully insisted upon by the Board of Trade. Her complement of passengers, some seventy in all, sat up to their waists in warm Adriatic water, all traces of good humour gone, and unimpressed by the fact that the Cadet Officer sat high and dry on the cabin roof of his craft, extolling them, in his best Pangbourne manner, 'not to panic, all will be well!'

An orderly but uncomfortable transfer was made of the passengers to the 'penny bus', and slow strained return made to *Arcadia*, progress being impeded by the ignominious tow of the 'limousine' behind. Once there, and safely aboard, relief at their rescue was bolstered by the envy of those already aboard who saw it as a rare adventure, and their mood lightened.

One by one, each of the 'limousines' sank to the limits permitted by buoyancy tanks, and the two senior-most Cadets, one each to the 'penny buses', towed them one by one to the waiting davit falls. The 'penny buses', uncomfortably open to the elements as they were, nevertheless proved themselves as fine sea-boats, and the two of them had to finish the task of reuniting passengers with ship.

On almost the last run back to the ship, and holding the plunging, kicking boat alongside the tourist gangway with great difficulty, the Cadet heard a shout from the gangway head. He glanced briefly upward, as seas smashed yet again against his boat and spray lashed across his tense face. It was the Gangway Officer, fresh from his shower, and immaculate in dry white uniform.

'I say, bloke,' he shouted down the crack and clatter of wind and wave, 'will you take this bird ashore this trip – it's just flown onto the deck,' and he held aloft a frightened flapping gull.

'No I won't,' came the snarled response, 'chuck the bloody thing over the side.'

At that he gave the order to let go, and lurched and pounded his way shoreward for the last trip of an eventful day, his departure marked by shouts of laughter and cheers from watching passengers.

Sadly the Cadet Officer took no further part in the boat handling for the rest of the cruising season. Not as a reflection of his competence, but rather the fact that he had not sufficiently encouraged his passengers whilst awaiting rescue, by joining them in the water that was waist deep in his boat!

As in all of the P & O liners, the Second Officer was the Navigator, and cruising placed a heavy workload on his shoulders. As a consequence, he invariably had a Cadet allocated to his watch at sea, if for no other reason than to rub out pencilled position markings and course marks from used charts! On that particular night watch, the 12-4 or 'death watch', en route for Cannes, *Arcadia* overtook a cruiser of the American Navy, and the Navigator saw an opportunity to further involve his Cadet. By coincidence, both he and the Cadet were in the Royal Naval Reserve, so it came as no surprise to the Cadet when instructed to 'Call her up, and send a RPC for Cannes, if she's bound there.'

Having first established identities, and destination, the RPC or 'Request the pleasure of your company' was duly sent, the beam of the 10 inch signalling lamp leaping away from the starboard bridge wing in blazing morse, answered with clipped professional competence by the warship's duty yeoman. The American Navy would visit *Arcadia*'s wardroom in Cannes, as the two ships lay close to each other at anchor in the bay.

The American Navy was 'dry' in the sense that no alcohol was allowed on board, which was often reflected in over-indulgence whilst ashore on leave. A visit to *Arcadia* was no exception, and while the officers were taken off to the Wardroom, so the Ensigns (American equivalent to the British Midshipmen) were consigned to the Cadets to be looked after, and so they were. The 'D' Deck cabins were adequately stocked with beer, to the utter astonishment of the Ensigns, who lost no time in setting about the Allsops with gusto.

Some few hours later, a far more unsteady group of Americans eased their way down the starboard side gangway where an impatient Coxswain held his launch in readiness to take his highly respected officers back to their ship.

'Get your drunken asses down here fast, Sirs,' he intoned in his deep southern black drawl. 'I don't have all goddamn night!'

And so the cruising season continued to late August, the cold Nordic waters for the first time embraced within the Northern Cities Cruise, and a strange contrast to the heat of the Mediterranean.

Arcadia's bulk was dwarfed in the fjords of Norway, the sound of her steam whistle echoing eerily round the towering ramparts of the fjord sides as she slipped through the dark deep waters, whilst careful attention was paid by the Watch Cadet to the echo sounder trace, as it leapt upwards towards *Arcadia*'s hull only to fall away dramatically as the mountain range beneath the water showed its teeth.

Helsinki was a boating port, and an unusually long haul from ship to shore through unfamiliar water for all the Cadets. No Errol Flynn to enliven the run in, but a deep desire to prove to the quietly attentive Finns on the quayside that yes, the young men bringing cruising passengers ashore could handle their craft. No repeat here of the embarrassment felt at one particular Mediterranean boating port, where three 'limousines' had berthed, and then stopped their powerful engines. None would be restarted, until a mightily sarcastic

Engineer Officer was brought ashore by 'penny bus' to wave his magic screwdriver.

There was in *Arcadia* one further demonstration of social and hierarchical importance that was to sustain the Cadets in their career paths. Traditionally in the P & O, the Second Officer was the Senior of the Junior Officers, and as such it was unwritten law in the liners that he sat at the head of the officers' table in the First Class Restaurant.

Arriving for breakfast one morning, he found his seat occupied by a first-trip Stenographer, Woman/Female Assistant Purser as the rank was to become. He said nothing, and took another seat, assuming it to be an error made by her in ignorance. The following morning, she again occupied his seat as he arrived from the Bridge to take breakfast. He sat down to her right, and observed politely, 'You're sitting in my chair, and perhaps you'll be good enough to sit elsewhere in future.'

'I'm an officer, the same as you,' she bridled, flushing but defensively determined, and silence fell upon the other occupants of the table.

The Navigator thoughtfully took a slice of toast from the silver rack, and glanced at her.

'So you want to be considered as an officer, do you?' he enquired gravely.

'Certainly,' she triumphed.

'Well, pass the f . . . ing butter then,' he snapped, at which the embarrassed girl burst into tears and fled the restaurant. This was fortunately between cruises, so no passengers were on board!

Southampton would be the final cruise port that August, and for the Cadets much frantic attention to a correspondence course to be completed prior to the cruise-end. Training had to go on in preparation for the first professional examination, the Second Mate's Certificate of Competency, and three at least among *Arcadia*'s complement of six Cadets were drawing close to the end of their Indentures.

As in *Iberia*, *Arcadia*'s Cadets prevailed upon the ship's printer to print invitation cards for a farewell gathering in the Wardroom, and one was despatched to every officer aboard, to include the Commanding Officer. As in *Iberia* the occasion was graced by the Captain

and those of his officers who were off-duty, for that was the way of
P & O.

'Finished with main engines,' intoned the Captain, preparing to
leave the Bridge after berthing in Southampton.

'Finished with main engines, Sir,' echoed the Officer of the Watch.

'Finished with main engines, Sir,' repeated the Cadet of the
Watch, and swung the brass handles of the ship's telegraph appropriately. The Season was over.

He was large, fat and extremely pompous. He was the P & O Shore
Chief Steward, and he was addressing a group of Officers and Cadets
gathered at Leadenhall Street during what was known as 'Group
Week', a communication exercise designed to bond ship and shore
staff together. He was not doing very well, and had largely alienated
his audience by his pomposity.

'Any questions?' he enquired, glancing impatiently at his expensive
watch.

'Is it true, Sir,' enquired one attendant Cadet fresh from cruising,
'that P & O operates a wing and leg farm?'

'What do you mean,' asked Sir, sensing that this was not to be
straightforward.

'Well, Sir, it seems that when we order chicken, we only get a
wing or a leg, but no breast.'

The Chief Steward relaxed, and replied in patronising manner,

'That may well be the case in the cargo ship fleet, but if and when
you aspire to the liners, you will find that we only serve breast in the
restaurants. What was your last appointment?'

'*Arcadia*, Sir!'

Nine years later, one of *Arcadia*'s Cadets was himself Navigator of
Orcades, during the Mediterranean cruising season. Inspired by *Iberia*,
Arcadia and an off-duty glass, he penned the following, without pause
or consideration for the finer points of poetry.

Ode to a Cruising Ship

Near sleek, near white and sometimes pounds, not in Sterling but in
   weathered weight
Not young, gets older, pushing time, seeking people, human freight,

Always forward up and down, costs and engines, turning round
In circles great or steers a line not too defined for one to sea,
Involved in keeping Watch and time, livelihood near sanity.
Within the bowels vast movements form, passing miles whilst up
   above
For want of womb, the bearing comes from land and eye caused not
   by love but sheer necessity!
In alley veins her life blood lives formed with cells for human bode
Some First, more not, and all injected there by different mode
But oft as not by plasma drip of honeyed words from practised lips of
   Advertising Housemen!
In calmer waters bounding on, by stern all trimmed and mouth afoam
Sometimes ensnared by Nature's shroud of fog, and gives two minute
   moans of mournful dirge, cacophony, decreed by Law and
   Ministry.
The end must come deprived of life, her lines all out umbilical
In rest rejoined to her Earth for few short hours, at least until
Adrenalin in human form, intent in seeking garlic sun
Pours to her heart which in its turn, responds and takes her out again.

Uncle George was splendidly avuncular in his good wishes to
Cadets for success in examinations, and W.A. Mackenzie, despite the
passage of three years, was still only able to sign himself as Acting
Secretary. Sign he did, however, beneath the collective wisdom of
P & O Steam Navigation Co. enscribed thus:

> We hereby certify that this Indenture has been completed to our
> entire satisfaction, the within mentioned Cadet having been reported
> upon by the Captains under whom he has served to be of very good
> conduct, ability and sobriety. We further certify that 4/5th of the time
> has been spent at sea
> > Peninsular & Oriental Steam Navigation Company
> > Acting Secretary.

After three interminable months at the Sir John Cass Nautical
College in London, resident in the depths of London's East End,
came the dreaded entry to the Board of Trade examination hall. This
was situated in Ensign Street off Dock Street, an area as culturally
impoverished as could be found. The area seemed a suitable
examination venue for those who had to sail in and out of Britain's

grimy and grim docklands, and there was no more suitable a place to portray the message 'abandon hope all ye who enter here'.

The Chief Examiner, conducting the oral examination of the would-be officer in his office, only shortly removed from the glass domed 'writtens' examination hall, was a diminutive but evil looking figure.

'P & O, eh? Spent most of your time on the bloody Bridge, I suppose,' he growled. 'Very well, Boy, describe to me a derrick heel block!'

'Well, Sir,' came the thoughtful response, 'it's red.'

Index

bold numbers indicate plates

Aberdeen, Hong Kong 96
abseiling 43
Adelaide 140, 156
Aden 3, 50, 55
Aden 75, 87, 90, 140–3
Admiralty House 35
Allan **40**
Alphonso 151–3
Andaman Islands **19**
Anderson, Sir Donald **1**, 39, 83
Anglesey, Marquis of 8, 9, 11, 41
Arabian Sea 76
Arcadia 2, 78, 96, 100, 109, 110, **32**, **34**, **35**, 122, 123, 156, 160–7, 168
Athens 135
Atkinson, K.I. **12**
Australasia 55, 57
Australian Bight 156

Ballarat 3, 55
Barclay Curle 61
barman 115–16
Bartram, Senior Cadet Captain **4**, **12**
Bass Strait 156
Batten, D. **8**
Bay of Biscay 75
Bayliss, Mr K. **8**
beer 67
Bendigo 3, 55
Bengal, Bay of 83
betelnut 82
Billy the Budgie 64
Bishop, Cadet **24**
Black Jack 114
Board of Trade 106

Bombay 143–4
British India Line 1, 79
Brocklebank Line 79
Brook-Smith, Lt-Commander 24

Calcutta 79–83
Camp, the 28
Canary Islands 111
Canberra 39, 128
Cannanore 3, 55, 61–87, **16**
Cannes 111, 130–1, 135
Canton 2, 96
Cape Leewen 156
Cape St Vincent 147
Captain Superintendent 37
Carthage 2
Ceylon (Sri Lanka) 77
Changi jail 92
Chappell, J.I. **12**
Chitral 92–3, 96
Christie, D.O. **8**
Chrysanthemum 136–7
Chusan 2, 78, 96
City Airport **15**
Clan Line 79
Cobra Island 86
cocktail party **30**, 136, **42**
Cocos Islands 140
Cole, W. **12**
Colombo 76, 77–8, 87, 90–1, 140
colour test 53
Conway Grace 16–17
Conway, HMS 4, 5, 7, 8–42, 43, **2**, **3**, 83, 106, 123
Corfu 2

Coromandel 3, 55, 61, 78
correspondence course 59, 65
cricket **23**, **24**, 92–3, 113
Crossing of the Line 140
Cubbin, R.J. **12**
Cunard Line 1, 135
Currie, Sir William 83
cutter 25

Dale, Senior Cadet Captain B.S. **4**, **8**, **12**
dance 90–1
Davie, Cadet Officer **17**, **18**, **26**, **27**, **40**, **41**, **43**
demerit 30
Devanha 3, 55, 78
dinner, formal 37
Discharge Book 53
Djakarta 145
dockers 89–90
Dongola 3, 55
Douglas, R.W. **8**, **11**, **12**
Drake, Chief Officer G. 13, 16
Dubrovnik 111, 162–3
Duff, Douglas V. 31
Dutton, H. **8**, **12**

Elder Dempster Lines 1
elephant **19**, 86
Empire Fowey 2
Empire Paragon 138, 141
Errington, Mr 49, 51, 63, 71, 87, 101–1, 148, 159
Errol Flynn 120
executive induction 23
'Extra' Certificate 20, 38

Falkner **32**, **35**
Fancy Dress dances 124, 152
Feasey, D.P. **12**
Ferguson, Cadet **24**, **26**
Finland 161
First Class 120–2
flag ceremony 78

Flying Angel Club 80
Formosa (Taiwan) 96
Fremantle 140, 156

Gala Night 124, 126
Gibbins, A.N. **12**
Gibraltar 111, 135
Gibraltar, Strait of 147
Gill, A.R. **8**
Goddard **26**
Grant, B. **11**, **12**
Grapenuts 44
Great Dane 63, 74–5
Green and Silley Weirs 106

Hamilton, Bermuda 111
Harland & Wolf 107
Harrington **26**, **27**, **40**, **41**, **43**
Harvey **26**
Hayes, B. **12**
Helsinki 166
Himalaya 2, 96
HM Customs 100
Holmes, 1st Officer **27**
Holmes, G.E.N. **5**, **11**, **12**
home leave 26
Hong Kong 56, 94–6
Honshu 96
Hoogli River 80–1
Hooley, D.S. **12**
Houghton, D.J. **12**
Hufflett, C.C. **12**
Hughes, T. **12**

Iberia 2, 78, 91, 96, 100, 105–36, **26**, **27**, **28**, **32** 168
Iberians skiffle group **43**, 126, 156, 157
Indefatigable, HMS 41
Indentures 47–8, 167
India 55, 57
Indian Ocean 133, 151
Indian Union strike 143, **38**
Interview Board 35
Ionian Sea 162

Islam, S.M.A. **11**, **12**
Ismir 135

jabs 36
Jimmy's Kitchen 96
Johns **26**
Jones, 1st Officer **27**
Journey's End 21, 31

Kandy 79
Kaohsiung 96
Karmala 3, 55
Kemp, Biff 108, **31**, 128
Kendal mint cake 44
King George V Dock 56–7, 61, **14, 15**, 100, 136
Kobe 96, 97
Kos 111, 135
Kowloon 95
Kyber 3, 55

Lane **32, 35**
Langridge, W.N. **12**
Las Palmas 111, 135
Laverick, G.M. **8**
Leadenhall St 49, 144, 148, 153, 157, 159, 168
Lifeboat Certificate 110
limousine **29**, 120, 161, 163–5
Lisbon 111, 135
Liverpool Sailors Home 6
Llanedwan 29
Lucas **26**

Mackenzie, W.A. 169
Madeira 111, 135
Madras 79, 83–4
Malacca, Strait of 90, 92
Malaga 111
Malaya 56
Malim Sahib's Hindustani, The 50
Maloya 128
Manley Road Swimming Club 93
Marsland, Cadet **24**

Martin, F. **11**, **12**
matron 36
Mavity, B.G. **8**
May, J.M. **8**
McGarr, N.K. **11**, **12**
McWalter, D.D. **12**
meals 67
Melbourne 156
Menai Bridge 8, 40
Menai Strait 8, 29, 39
Menzies, Sir Robert Gordon 162
Merchant Navy Defence Course 136
merit-half day 30
Messina Strait 162
Minikoy 76
Mission for Seamen 80
Morning Departure 21, 39
Morris, C.E. **12**
Munro, I.C. **8**, **12**

Naples 111, 135
New Chums 12, 13–15, 18, 26
Nile, HMS 8

Oakes, R.N.E. **12**
Orcades 96, 168
Oriana 132–3
Orient Line 1
Orme **11**, **12**
Oronsay 96
Orsova 96
Outward Bound Trust **13**, 43–6
Owen, J.H. **11**, **12**

P & O 1, 2, 34, 46–8, 49, 55, 95, 138–9 & passim
P & O Regulations 58
Padre 21–2, 38
Palethorpe sausage 28
Palma 111, 135
Pangbourne 4, 5, 20, 43, 64, 106, 123
parade training 24
Paston, Cadet **18**
Patonga 157

Patonga 3, 55, 79
pea-shooter 148
Peartree **26**
Penang **23**, 91
Peninsular & Orient Steam Navigation
    Company (P & O) 1, 2, 34, 46–8,
    49, 55, 95, 138–9 & passim
penny bus 161, 163–5
Perim 3, 55
Perry, J.W. **1**, **4**, **11**, **12**, **13**, **18**, **24**, **26**,
    27, **32**, **35**, **40**, **41**, **43** & passim
Phipps, T.I.H. **8**
Pickup, P. **11**, **12**
pilots 72, 75, 81–2, 93, 100, 112
Pinjarra 3, 55, 91, 138–42, **36**
Plas Newydd 10, 14, 27, 29, 30–1, 35,
    42, **7**
Pollitt, Capt. 110
Port Arthur 157
Port Blair 85
Port of London Authority 56
Port Said 70
Port Sudan 87
Porteous **32**, **35**
Potsdam 2
prickly heat 90
Pritchard, B.E. **8**
Puddifer, E.G. **8**
Purfina Congo 74, 101

Quarter Boys 12, 13, 27, 30, 40
Queen of Bermuda 119

Raffles Hotel 93
Rahman, Q.A.B.M.M. **11**, **12**
Rajula **20**, 84–5
Red Sea 74, 87, 151
Red Sea rig 95
Redman, D.A. **12**
Redmond, S. **12**
Repton, HMS 118
Roberts, D.A. **12**
Rommel 21, 29
Ronuk 27, 42, 63

Rotterdam 145–6
Royal Albert Dock **14**, **15**, 56–7
Royal Mail Line 1
Royal Naval Reserve 35
rugby 20
Ruys 69

S.W. Silver & Co 49, 51, 84, 101, 126,
    129
Safmarine Lone 135
Sailors' Home 49
Scirroco 120
Secunny 61–2
Senior **32**, **35**
Serang 76
Shanghai 98–9
Sharp, J.W. **12**
Sheriff of Deadwood 32
Shillong 3, 56, 74, **21**, **22**, 88–100
signals 69–70
Sinclair, A.G. **12**
Singapore 3, 56, 88
Singapore 56, 91–3
Singapore Swimming Club 93
Sinkinson **11**, **12**
Sir James Laing shipbuilders 138
Sir John Cass Nautical College 169
skiffle group 'Iberians' **43**, 126, 156,
    157
Skinner, Chief Petty Officer 24
Slee, C.H.V. **11**, **12**
Socotra 3, 55. 76
Somali 3, 56, 88
Soovere, T. **8**
Soudan 3, 56, 88
Southampton 134, 167
Speed, A.J. **12**
Split 161
Sri Lanka (Ceylon) 77
St Mark's Square, Venice 129–30
Star Ferry 96
Stern, Cadet **13**
stewards 117–18
Strathaird 2, 70, 141–52, **37**, **40**, **41**

Strathallan 2, 159
Stratheden 2, 78, 159
Strathmore 2, 159
Strathnaver 2, 78, 159
Suez Canal 70, 151, 154
Sukarno, President 145
Sumatra 90
Surat 3, 56, 88
Sunda 3, 56, 88
Sunday Divisions **9**
Swanson, Chief Cadet Captain A.J.M. **1**, **4**, **8**, **11**, **12**
Sydney 156–7
Sydney Ball 156

Taiwan (Formosa) 96
Tanglin Club 93
Tavender, Cadet **24**
teaser 15, 17–18, 29
Tenerife 111, 112
Tilbury Docks 56–7, 105–10, 149, 161
Tourist Class 120–2
Turner, J.A. **11**, **12**, **40**

Ullswater, Lake 43, 46
uniform 1, 6, 23, 49–52, 66, 71, 74, 84, 90, 101–4, 126–9, 141, 148
Union Castle Line 135
Urdu 113–14

Venice 111, 129–30
Victoria Dock 56–7
Vigo 111, 135
Vishakhapatnam 79

Wallin, G.P. **11**, **12**
Warsash School of Navigation 4, 5, 43, 106, 123
Warship, HM 76
washing up plates 118–19
watches 65, 67, 68–9, 113
Watson, I.G. **11**, **12**
Whillance, Cadet **24**
Whitehouse, J.P. **12**
Wilhelm van Oldebarneveldt 69
Wilkin **40**
Wilkins, J.M.M. **12**
Willi **32**, **35**
Wilson, D.F. **12**
Woods, D.W. **11**, **12**
Worcester, HMS 4, 5 , 20, 43, 64, 106, 123

Yangste Kiang River 98
Yokohama 96
Yugoslavia 161–2